At The Crossroads:
A Vision Of Hope

At The Crossroads:
A Vision Of Hope

Bishop Thomas G. Doran

At the Crossroads: A Vision of Hope is compiled and edited into book form by John Gile from more than 900 pages of writings and transcriptions of speeches by Bishop Thomas G. Doran.

At The Crossroads: A Vision Of Hope

Bishop Thomas G. Doran

10   9   8   7   6   5   4   3   2

Library of Congress Card Number: 00-100855
ISBN: 0-910941-26-2

Published by JGC/United Publishing Corps
Rockford, Illinois

Cover photograph by Jeff Arns
Cover design by Debbie Taft-Heather

Produced in the United States of America
by Worzalla, Stevens Point, Wisconsin

Foreword

Why This Book?
Why This Author?

At the Crossroads: A Vision of Hope is about our future, about our rights, relationships, and responsibilities, about making life better and happier.

Today's children are growing up in a world with values very different from those most adults knew as children. When I was a child, I could ride my bicycle anywhere, leave it unlocked outside, and find it there when I came back. I could walk anywhere in my home town day or night without fear. And I certainly was safe in school. Now the values and principles which fostered that respect for life and property have declined and many freedoms we enjoyed just a few years ago are being lost to restrictions and precautions required to safeguard ourselves and our children from human predators.

There seems to be a double standard at work when it comes to dealing with the moral pollution which has been steadily eroding our human freedoms.

Environmental pollution was met with outrage and determination to overcome it. Today we breathe cleaner air and drink cleaner water because we resolved to change. But moral pollution which diminishes joy and destroys lives often is met with resignation. Many shrug and say, "We can't do anything about it." *At The Crossroads: A Vision Of Hope* reminds us that we need not accept foul contaminants which corrupt our spirit any more than we need accept foul contaminants which choke and poison our bodies.

At The Crossroads: A Vision Of Hope is unique in its perspective because it is the work of a history teacher and lawyer who happens to be a priest and bishop. It provides, therefore, a broad view which combines what could be called the best of both worlds. It is not a theoretical treatise, but a prescription for change, starting with you and me.

The author, as you will see for yourself in the pages which follow, is a man of both profound intellect and deep compassion. Publishing his work is a privilege, an honor, and a joy.

John Gile
Editor and Publisher

Introduction

Americans enjoy political freedoms which are the envy of citizens in other nations. But there is a greater, higher, broader, deeper form of freedom which is the foundation for political freedom and without which political freedoms cannot continue to exist. It is a freedom which inspires us to rise above self-absorption and is manifest in personal honor and integrity. Some say many Americans are losing sight of that more profound form of freedom — and are destroying the very basis for our political freedoms in the process.

At The Crossroads: A Vision Of Hope is an antidote for the erosion of those values and ideas which undergird our freedoms. It is a prescription to enrich our lives and the lives of others. May it be for you a source of understanding, strength, confidence, and joy.

Contents

Recall Cain's answer to the question, "Where is your brother?" He replied, "Am I my brother's keeper?" With that, he became the spokesperson for a perverse idea of freedom that today has led some to accept unbridled selfishness and even crimes against humankind as legitimate expressions of individual freedom.

What Is Real Freedom?

There is a big difference between the way southern European people and northern European people express the concept which we in America talk about as "freedom." All of the Latin peoples — the Italians, the Spanish, the Portuguese, the French, the Romansch, the Catalan, the Provençal — use for that expression a word derived from the Latin "liber, libertas." And to be free, "liber," to enjoy liberty, was to pass from a state of childhood to a state of adulthood.

Children, adolescents, were not in the strict sense free. They were under the power of their fathers, which could be terrible. The Romans, remember, were pagans and the father of a family had the absolute right of life and death over his children. I am sure that those of you who have studied any Roman

3

history are aware that Roman fathers occasionally, when there were children who were born deformed or deficient or female, which to the Romans was the same thing, would decide to expose them on the hills around Rome, letting them be eaten by rodents and wild animals. All the sane, sober Roman writers, even the early ones, would say that practice was not right, in the sense of the right thing to do, but they would agree that it was his right under Roman law to do it.

So children were not free. They were under the absolute power of their parents. What liberty meant was to assume responsibility. When you became free, you had the right to pay taxes. With your liberty came the right to do public service. Liberty meant you had all the privileges and all the burdens or responsibilities of citizenship. And, to a greater or lesser degree, those peoples have preserved that idea of liberty.

In the German nations, however, the concept of freedom was what we regard as free in "born free" — an animal-like freedom. The animal is to remain untrammeled. It is to be subject to no restrictions. It does whatever it pleases.

The two ideas are very different. Somehow we have managed to preserve both. We speak of our country as a nation with "liberty and justice for all," not "freedom and justice for all." Thomas Jefferson, George Washington, Benjamin Franklin, and their peers were too smart for that. They knew that the freedom of the animal world would never work for a human society, so they talked about liberty in the Declaration of Independence and the Constitution.

Gradually, the concept of animal-like freedom advocated by philosophers such as John Locke and John Dewey has become a part of some Americans' mindsets and even has penetrated our educational system. It is expressed simply as, "I should not be subject to any restrictions." Now, if you think about it, no human society is possible on that basis.

"I am free to do what I want with my own body," for example, is a proposition that sounds good, but is it true? Pushed to its ridiculous extreme, it would mean that if someone took out a rifle and started shooting at children on a playground, he or she could justify it by saying, "All I'm doing is exercising my trigger finger. Am I not free to do what I want to do with my own hand?"

When we consider human freedom, the operative word is the word "human." Human freedom is a freedom that enables you to do what is right, to follow your conscience. That conscience, if it is nourished by proper parental example, good education, and positive motivation, will yield what was the ideal of our nation's founders, the law abiding person.

A law abiding person is different from a law obedient person. A law obedient person is the person who is zipping along at 85 and hits the brakes when he sees one of those cars with the red and blue lights. He goes smiling by the trooper and then, when the trooper recedes into the rear view mirror, BINGO, the pedal hits the metal and he is back into the take-off mode. That is mere observance of the law, the law obedient or law observing person.

The law abiding person, on the other hand, is a person who appreciates the law and welcomes it. Why? It is because law abiding persons know that wise and just human laws — and we will explore the basis for laws which are wise and just later — are enacted out of love. Why is traffic in a congested, residential area restricted to 30 miles per hour? Wise humans know it is because if we all abide by that law, fewer people will be injured and die on that street.

The law abiding person respects and is concerned about the well being of others and of our larger communities. Another word for that respect and concern which provide the basis for human freedom is love. On the following pages, we will explore the origin of and rationale for that love which is the very foundation of a society with liberty and justice for all.

The common good is the sum total of social conditions which allow people either as groups or individuals to reach their fulfillment more fully and more easily. If we could work toward a notion of the common good in this country, we would be closer than we are to the Jeffersonian ideal of democracy. We also would be a lot closer, though not all the way, to what Jesus meant when he said, "Love one another as I have loved you."

Defenders Of Freedom

Some see the world as a battleground where two opposing forces wage war. They applaud advocates of virtually unrestrained self-indulgence as noble defenders of freedom and condemn all who oppose them. They forget or ignore the reality that our human freedoms paradoxically hinge on self-restraint and that unbridled self-indulgence ultimately destroys freedom. In their delusion, they vilify the real defenders of freedom and tear down the very principles and institutions which preserve human dignity, safeguard liberty, and point the way to joy-filled living.

Some difficulties identifying the real defenders of freedom stem from popular misunderstandings and misconceptions fostered by well-intentioned but poorly informed media. Consider, for example, how the mass media, deliberately or unwittingly espousing the religions of secularism and atheism, treat a primary guide to human freedom and happiness — the Ten Commandments.

It is very important that we begin with a proper understanding of what the Commandments are designed to do. Otherwise, we fall into the shallow type of religious analysis which says, "Well, God is just a meddler and religion is only a matter of telling you what thou shalt not do." Those who think that way have it all backwards. The purpose of God's Commandments is one long act of love.

If you look at the Ten Commandments all together, they are the basis upon which any orderly and peaceful society can live. No society can survive if those simple precepts are not observed. If we do not have domestic peace which derives from honoring one's parents, if we cannot stop killing each other, if the family is not sacred, if property is not sacred, if we cannot trust one another with the truth, if we are constantly envious and jealous of one another, there will not be a happy society. No happy society can exist with a horde of people who are ingrates towards their parents and who are killers and adulterers and thieves and liars and are constantly looking to get the other person's property and wife. It just cannot work.

We are made as human beings to live in society. A society is a group of persons bound together by a principle of unity that goes beyond each one of them. It is a characteristic of human beings down through history that we form societies, clans, tribes, labor guilds and unions, nations, states, religious groups, civic groups, groups for mutual assistance, groups for entertainment, sports groups, whatever. In the Book of Genesis, we are told that, when Adam was alone, God said, "This is not good," and created woman to be the partner of man. "It is not good for man to be alone" goes beyond the relationship of men and women, goes beyond the family to cover every facet of our lives. We require other people. They make us whole.

Now, it is true each community is defined by its purpose and, consequently, obeys specific rules. But in all true and healthy human societies, the well being of the human person is and ought to be the subject and the end of all its institutions. We have been through a lot which violated that principle in the last few decades. We have experienced human societies which did not keep the human person as its principal subject and end. We have had the collectivist societies of national socialists, Nazism and Fascism. And we have had Communism. When we compare the characteristics of those totalitarian political systems, we see that Fascism, Nazism, and Communism are essentially the same thing. What do they have in common? They say, "The most important thing in any society is the society."

Our Judeo-Christian society differs. We give Thomas Jefferson a lot of credit for writing, "We hold these truths to be self-evident: that all men are created equal," but that was first said centuries earlier by a Cardinal in Italy, Saint Robert Bellarmine. In describing what makes for a truly human society, Bellarmine went on to say that everyone, every human being, is endowed by God with certain rights which cannot be taken away — that is, rights which are unalienable — and among them are the right to life, and the right to liberty — not freedom, but liberty — and the pursuit of happiness. The human person, the human individual, the

14

human being is the basis of society, not a cog in it or a piece of it. That is why Judeo-Christian society says, "What is most important in a truly human society is the human person."

Obviously, we cannot all create our own sewage departments and our own fire departments or post office departments, so human beings have to form societies in order to get those types of things done. In so doing, it also is important to resist the tendency which is all too common in human life to let somebody else do everything, to cast all of our hopes and all of our fears on somebody else. The principle of subsidiarity holds that no higher society should do what a lower one can. In other words, no society or government should do what the individual can do for himself or herself. That is to preserve each person's dignity and promote the good of society. Those things which individuals cannot do for themselves, the next higher level of the social organization should do. That is how a healthy, balanced society functions.

There is a certain solidarity in human communities which hold that the well-being of every person is their first and foremost concern and which are made up of individuals who have helping one another as their goal. All societies must have this in them or they fail, as we have seen time and time again throughout history. But how does the individual go about contributing to the social integrity of the community? We could do it as a catch as catch can, I suppose. That would be one way, the only way if we had nothing more than the primitive powers of mere rationalistic or naturalistic religion. The Judeo-Christian wellspring of our liberty, however, flows from our relationship with a Creator who not only endows us with unalienable rights, but whose self-revelation includes life-enriching instructions for us. One part of those instructions is the Ten Commandments. They tell us how to relate to our Creator and each other with love, how to grow in love. It is as though God says through the Commandments, "Look, here are some basic rules. If you follow them, your life will be a lot less troublesome and a lot more enjoyable." That is what the Commandments are.

The Commandments are worded the way they are so that we will not fall into difficulty. They are a set of laws, and you can word laws two ways. You can say, "You ought to do this, that, thus, and so." That is one way laws are worded. Another way is to say, "You shall not do this, that, thus, and so." In our language, in our thought patterns, you see, negative laws bind always and forever. "Thou shalt not do these things," means never, with no exception. The negative wording of the Commandments makes them clear and easy for us to understand.

The Ten Commandments are the prescription, the basis, the common matter of all human living. Our human nature is endowed with conscience, the faculty to know almost automatically, almost instinctively, what is right and what is wrong. You will find some of the Ten Commandments in all the systems of morality that have been thought up by men and women down through history. What about Moses with two tablets of the law then, what was that? It is as though God, in his love for us, said, "Look, I know that you might get some of these, but you won't get all of them, so I'm going to write it out for you." That is what the Commandments are. If you look at them in the clear and sober light of day, you will see that there is not much in them that does not respond to our inner nature and our common sense.

No society ever existed or can exist with indigenous murder. In order for people to get along, we have to say, "Our first rule: don't kill each other, don't do violence to one another." Someone might say to you, "Well, that's common sense." Exactly. That is why God gave us the Commandment.

"You shall not commit adultery," is another. Adultery has become, on daytime TV, a major indoor sport. But see what it has done to our society in the process. It has smashed the family. It has ground up children. The reason why you have children now out on the streets with guns killing people is because they have been betrayed. And that betrayal is the betrayal that starts with unfaithfulness in the home. In order to be able to grow up a healthy human being, you must be able to trust somebody. The first people we depend on and from whom we learn to trust are mom and dad. If they cannot trust each other, how can they pass on a trusting society to their children? Someone might say, "Well, that's just common sense." Right. That is why God gave us the Commandment.

"You shall not steal," is another. If everyone is stealing everybody else's

18

property, you get constant war. You cannot have that, so God said, "Don't steal."

"You shall not bear false witness against your neighbor," is another. All human relationships depend on trust. My entering into a useful relationship with you demands that I be able to take you at your word and you be able to take me at mine. Lying destroys trust, so God says, "Don't lie."

If we are constantly wanting what belongs to others and saying, "Oh, if only I had that wife or husband, if only I had that property, if only I had this car, if only I had this, if only I had that," we do not keep our minds on living our own lives. Lives of envy and jealousy are not human. And so God says, "Don't covet." Someone might say, "Well that makes perfect sense." Yes, it does. That is why God gave it to us.

Of course, compared to those simple Commandments, the other four are absolutely beautiful. "I am the Lord your God, you shall not have strange gods before me." "You shall not take the name of the Lord in vain." "Remember to keep holy the Lord's Day." "Honor your father and your mother."

What are the Ten Commandments? Prohibitions? Strict rules? God trying to get us and make us do what he wants? No. He is trying to make us happy, and when we follow those simple rules, human society becomes happy. That becomes crystal clear when you answer this question: if everyone on earth, all six billion people, kept the Ten Commandments, do you think this would be a worse world or a better one?

There is a society that is the wealthiest in the world, but where there are vast gaps between the rich and the poor. It is terrorized by urban crime and street gangs in some places. Its government is somewhat and seemingly hopelessly corrupt. There is no religious influence. It has an outdated educational system and is plagued by urban blight and decay, dissolute living, unstable family life, and widespread drug abuse. There is a high suicide rate, rampant divorce, and burgeoning welfare. Athletics are glorified and expensive. It has the greatest legal system in the world, a huge defense and armament industry, and imposes its system of government on foreign lands. Abortion is commonplace and the status of women there grows worse by the day. The society I am talking about is not ours. It is the Roman Society at the time of Augustus and Tiberius Caesar, and it died, it just fell apart.

Transcending Change

Because the world as we know it is passing away, we are living in a time which will produce great change. Some would have us believe that change is an absolute value. When political arguments develop, we often hear, "Oh, this one is good because he or she is for change." Or we hear the president say, in naming people for some award, "We are honoring these men and women because they are agents for change."

People for whom change is the only thing that matters are like the famous character Captain Nemo, captain of the submarine in Jules Verne's story *Twenty Thousand Leagues Under The Sea*. Nemo is a Latin word for nobody. No one. His motto was "mobilis in mobili," that is "changing in change." And, of course, who was he? He had no identity. He had no place. He had no purpose. He had no mission. He had no message. He had no goal. He had no end. He was one of the saddest characters in all of literature.

As Americans, we have a myth to which we cling — and there is nothing wrong with clinging to it as long as we realize it is a myth — of the necessary upward progress of everything. We have always been optimistic, and we believe that change is for the better. But we know in our heart of hearts that some changes are for the worse. In biology and medicine, we know many changes occur in human physical structure throughout life. One change which can occur is cancer. Cancer is a physical change, but not a physical change for the better.

In some very important and painfully obvious ways, you could say our surrounding society is suffering from a cancer, is devolving, changing for the worse. It is as though the world has almost turned on its head. We accept things in contemporary society that we know in the depths of our being are terribly, terribly wrong, and we do not want to talk about them. If a child is inconvenient before it is born, kill him, kill her, but do not call it killing, call it abortion. If a person lives beyond the years when the doctor and society consider that person to be useful, kill him, kill her, but do not call it killing, call it euthanasia. The single greatest cause of death, I am told, for people under 25 in our country today is suicide. If life gets too difficult, kill yourself, but do not call it killing.

Up until the last four or five years in the United States, no matter what murders went on, no matter what violence, no matter what savagery, it was unheard of that a child should kill a child or anyone else. Unheard of. And now it is commonplace. I can never remember a rash of kidnappings and murders of children such as we have today. This is not something that happens by chance. This happens because we have devalued life. And our children have picked that up. Children imitate what they see in the society around them. That is what prompted Pope John Paul II to issue an encyclical or letter to us in which he called our contemporary world culture a "culture of death" and urged us to realize our power to rise above it.

Even our Justice System manifests serious signs of decline — to the point that a recent survey reported less than twenty percent of American people, fewer than one in five, believe our Justice System is honest or just or fair. The report suggests we have created a judiciary at the federal and at some state levels which gives to judges powers that even the British King was not claiming for himself when we revolted more than two hundred years ago. We say "with liberty and justice for all," but many say it has come down to liberty and justice only for the rich, while others are victimized by judges' arbitrary decisions and are left with no recourse. We do not have to accept that.

Another change that is not for the better is the bleak forecast that, despite pockets of prosperity, our children and their children will become the first generations in American history to experience a declining quality of life. We see in our society around us that our nation and our big cities border on becoming ungovernable. We have a government dominated school system that now in twelve years of so-called education does not succeed in teaching people what most children learned in their first two years of school just a decade or two ago. We have so many,

many people in our country who are not able to read and write — more than 50 million according to some studies. We do not have to accept any of that.

Because of the rapid and radical cultural transformations which we are witnessing, some have called the time in which we live an interstitial time, a period between ages. The changes and turbulence can be very distressing for those who have a limited view and understanding of human history, but the experience is neither new nor disconcerting in the eyes of the Church. The Church is an institution twice as old as the second oldest institution in our western world. It spans 2,000 years and it has prospered in every age. If at times its institutions and its forms seem to decline, those forms reawaken and flourish in other times. That is because the Church has always stood for a solid system of values which is transcendental, that is, it transcends the ordinary changes of time and place, politics, economics, and education. It goes beyond that which we look for in ordinary society.

The Church goes on as societies collapse and die. When European society collapsed in the fourth century, in the eleventh century, and in the sixteenth century, virtually everything which was there passed away — except the Church. We have no doubt as to what is going to happen. We know that to this society must succeed another, since nothing material does not break up, break down, dissolve, rot, decay. But we do have a concern for all those who will suffer discouragement, disillusionment, and despair if our civil society, because of a disregard for the gift of life, because of a disregard for the gospel of life, fails to fulfill its potential.

I am not a pessimist. I believe we can make a difference. We can, by our practice of virtue, however you wish to define it, as the Greeks or the Romans, as the Judeo-Christians or whatever, our practice of what we consider virtue can overcome these things and make a happier, more congenial life for our fellows on this planet until they exit it in the normal course of events.

I invite you to explore with me on the following pages reasons for that hope. My optimism is based not on passing fads or wishful thinking, but on the timeless values and ideas which have sustained and do sustain us through all sorts of sociological and political and economic changes. If there is a chance to reverse some of the things that now seem to spell the end of our society as we know it, it is going to fall to each of us trying to achieve the ideals which are presented here and which can bring us back to some sort of reasonable, civil polity. Any effort we expend will be worth it when you consider the alternative.

In America, we do not have a common culture like the cultures that bind together the peoples in other nations. The only thing we have in common and the only thing we can rely on is the law. But law is a poor uniter of people. Remember this about law: law is outdated the day it is enacted. Why? Because legislators look at some situation they want to correct and say, "We don't want that happening in the future," so they make a law to correct the situation. But that same situation may never occur in the future. Or it may occur in a different way which is not precisely covered by the law. So you see where we are when we say we have no recourse in dealing with moral or ethical or medical or educational or economic or social problems other than the law. Law is for settling arguments. It is not for forging a people.

Finding A More Realistic
And Reliable Standard

The fully human life can be compared to a beautiful mosaic with all its varicolored pieces cut precisely to fit its design, its scope, its form. But take away a few pieces and see what happens. Other pieces begin to shift and slip and fall out. Soon you have nothing left of the original picture or design. That is similar to what happens to us as we lose the sense of our Judeo-Christian tradition. We lose our basis for and sense of human dignity. When our sense of human dignity is lost, there is also the tendency to deny God. And when God is out of our lives, all sorts of things happen.

Once you take God out of the picture, you destroy humanity because taking God out eliminates the spiritual aspect of our nature — which is the basis for truly human freedom — and puts all creatures on the same level. It reduces us to mere animals. Our Judeo-Christian heritage tells us that we are made in the image and likeness of God, that we have a spiritual as well as a physical nature, which gives us dignity and value, meaning and purpose.

Our intellect can discern that uniquely human quality in everyday life. Consider, for example, why an animal cannot be a criminal. If an animal, a tiger, leaps out of the bush and kills somebody, we may do something to protect other people from it, but we do not say that the tiger is a criminal. Why? Because the animal is an entirely material being. It acts according to its material instincts and does not see you as any different from a gazelle or a cow or a sheep. All it sees is lunch. So there is no such thing as murder for a carnivore. It simply acts according to its nature. But our human nature, yours and mine, is different. Our nature is partly material, resembling the nature of animals, and partly spiritual. Taking God out of the picture obscures that important difference and can lead us to the point, if we are not there already, where a baby seal is worth more than a baby human.

Once we take God out of the picture, we arrive at a practical materialism which leads us to individualism and utilitarianism and hedonism, none of which has ever elevated the human spirit in any age of which we know. The quality of life no longer includes the interpersonal, spiritual, or religious, but an exaggerated emphasis on the externals.

Much of our current American society is based on those externals. It is as though our society sits on a three-legged stool. One of the stool's legs, unfortunately, is materialism — the philosophy which says we are here for a short time and material things are all that matter. Grab as much as you can as fast as you can because that is all there is to life. The second leg of our society's three-legged stool is consumerism. We are bombarded day and night on the radio, the television, and all the other media with the idea that there is nothing in this world that we should not buy, that we do not need, that we should not want, that we cannot have. And the third pillar of that three-legged stool is, of course, individualism with its motto, "I alone am first, am most important, and I am first and most important all the time."

Taking God out of the picture has sent us on a false quest, a mistaken trip, a journey to nowhere. It has left many unable to see any purpose in human life beyond the frantic pursuit of an elusive happiness. They cannot even define happiness beyond whatever feels good at the moment. The result is confusion between good and evil — and diminished human freedom. That is why so many, many of our fellow humans have a slave-like existence. Materialism makes us slaves — slaves to public opinion, slaves to the tastes of the moment, slaves to the ideas of corrupt politicians, slaves to the television, slaves to whatever captivates us at the time.

Basing happiness on our material nature is a chase after the wind. Think of your own experiences. You say, "Oh, if only I had such and such, I would be happy." Then you get it, and what happens after time passes? It no longer makes you happy. You seek something new — which makes you happy for a while, until it, in turn, must be replaced by another novelty or trinket. We see the same in children who long for certain toys in October and November and December. They receive the toys for Christmas and are tired of them by

New Year's Day. That is not to say there is anything wrong with you or the children. That is just the way life is. We go from happiness to happiness, but no happiness which is bounded by time and space, no mere material happiness that we know of so far in human experience, lasts more than a little while.

Materialism, commercialism, and individualism replace God with little gods that govern our lives. Some people have a lust for power, money, beauty, sex, whatever — that becomes their god. Some may become workaholics. Then their god is work. Those little gods keep us from being truly human. They are not gods in the sense of the old polytheistic religions of the Greeks and Romans, but gods in the more authentic sense of what drives our lives.

Materialism, commercialism, and individualism are self-defeating because we can never get enough, are never satisfied, and some day we have to let go of everything. They breed cynicism and lowered expectations for ourselves and others as they eclipse the individual moral conscience and impair the moral conscience of our society. All of us are victimized now to the point where, for example, we may look at people who have the public trust and betray it, people who lie and cheat and steal, or people who are blatantly unfaithful and obscene, and we do not say, "Oh, how awful." We say, "What can you expect?"

That attitude is acknowledgment that we have created a somewhat deranged culture in which things are distracting us from what we are and hope to be. It is a sign of what we might call materialism addiction, of our becoming possessed by possessions. The Japanese have a saying about their rice wine saki. They say, "With the first glass, the man drinks the saki. With the second, the saki drinks the saki. And with the third and afterward, the saki drinks the man." That is true of every addiction. The obvious corruption and pollution of materialism challenge each of us to decide once and for all, am I going to be the ruler of my possessions, or are they going to rule me? We are being challenged to realize that maybe less is more. Maybe a simpler lifestyle is a better lifestyle.

The integration or balance of our material and spiritual nature is always something to which we have to devote conscious effort. Our instincts, material instincts, make us act and react as mere material beings, as animals. Our spiritual nature makes us act according to our spiritual nature. No truly human, fully human life can be lived on the merely material basis of our nature. We are made for more.

As Saint Augustine reminds us, "Our hearts were made for you alone, O Lord, and they are restless until they rest in you." With that in mind, we have a more realistic and reliable standard for evaluating the things of this world. Their worth is determined not by their intrinsic value, but by whether they bring us closer to or farther away from God. That which brings us into a more personal, more loving, more intimate relationship with God is more valuable. That which takes us out of that loving relationship is harmful.

The right and proper use of this world and this world's goods brings us into a deeper and closer relationship with God — and opens us to a deeper and closer relationship with each other. That is the message of hope and love which the Church brings to all.

Our spiritual nature demands more than material happiness which is limited by time and space. We see evidence of that as we look out upon our world and see people searching, searching, searching, going all over the earth, climbing, digging, diving, exploring, searching for some connection with the transcendent. Go to any book store and you will find all sorts of books on astrology and psychology and mind probing and depth analysis, all sorts of Eastern mysticism and Western monasticism. All of those things indicate how deep and how wide and how desperate is our search. Ironically, we are so focused and absorbed and preoccupied with it that we fail to realize we ourselves are being sought.

Let me illustrate what I mean. In 1989, one of the most devastating earthquakes in modern times leveled a town in the nation of Armenia. One widely reported account from the scene told of the father of a family who left his wife and daughter in a place of security and went to find his son. From the time his son was a little boy, the father had told him, "Whenever you need me, I'll be there for you. Whatever be the case, I will not desert you." He went to the school where his son had been in class that day and found the building leveled to the ground. After figuring out where in that building his son would have been, he started to dig away with his bare hands in the rubble. Other parents were there, too. Pretty soon they said, "It's hopeless. Give up." He said, "Are you going to help me or aren't you?" And he kept digging and digging and digging till his hands ran red with blood. The fire chief came and said, "Look, it's all over." And he said, "Are you going to help me or aren't you?" And he went on digging and digging and digging. Late in the afternoon the police chief came and said, "Listen, this is futile. You're just making a scene." And the father answered, "Are you going to help me or aren't you?" And he kept digging and digging and digging. People said, "He's a fool. He's crazy. He's mad." Then from out of the rubble came a voice, "Dad." He called his son's name and asked, "Are you safe?" His son answered, "Yes. There are fourteen of us down here." The father said, "Give me your hand, I'll pull you out." But his son said, "No, I'm not hurt. Take some of the others first." And he told his father, "Dad, I knew you'd come. I knew you would be there for me."

That is how God seeks us and says to all of us through the Church, "I am here for you always, at all times, no matter what." If there is one thing that is the best kept secret of Christianity, all branches, it is that God created this world and all that is in it, the entire universe, so that he would have the opportunity to love us. That is the whole purpose for God's creation. And the only thing God wants of us is to let him love us more. He has made an exception of no one, no one is excluded, abandoned, left outside. God knows our flawed nature, knows us better than we know ourselves, loves us in spite of our flaws, and has given us in the Church every help, every aid, every assistance, every advantage to help us respond to his love. Those helps all fit together in the Church like the beautiful mosaic mentioned earlier, locking together like the pieces of a puzzle which satisfies our search, our quest. We will now begin to explore those helps.

One thing about the Catholic faith is that it all hangs together. If you study it all, you've got a complete puzzle. It's not, "There's nothing down here in the corner, two or three pieces missing," or "One of them I had to cut to fit." No, it's all there and it all fits together.

Beginning With The Basics

The life-giving, life-sustaining, life-enriching helps we find in the Church match our nature and needs like the interlocking pieces of a puzzle, but seeing how they fit together requires a mature understanding of authentic Church teachings — and we dare not leave anything out. There always are some who want to omit one Church teaching or another or who want to focus on one and forget the others. That is why Historical Christianity is replete with rifts and shifts and schisms and splits that scramble the picture for us.

Perhaps the fastest and simplest way for us to begin understanding how it all fits together is to start with our creeds. The fact that various peoples and groups have different formulas to express their convictions and beliefs is familiar to us as Americans. We have, for example, our nation's Declaration of Independence in which we say, "We hold these truths to be self-evident: that all men are created equal; that they are endowed by their Creator with certain unalienable rights; that among these are life, liberty, and the pursuit of happiness." After that, of course, the Declaration sets forth the particular grievances which people down through the ages have always had against government. Those lists of rights, of fundamental truths, and of grievances make a sort of secular creed. They express a kind of formula by which we, as Americans, come to view our sociopolitical life. The Church has creeds for essentially the same reason.

The word "creed" comes from the Latin word "credo," which means "I believe." The two most basic creeds we have are the Apostles' Creed and the Nicene Creed. The first creed is called the Apostles' Creed because Church Tradition tells us that it was composed by the Apostles themselves after Jesus' Resurrection and before the Apostles dispersed from Jerusalem. The second is called the Nicene Creed because it was composed by the Council of Nicaea in the year 325.

You may ask, "Well, what prompted them in the year 325 to go over everything again? Wasn't the Apostles' Creed enough for them?" The question is interesting because it helps us understand how the Church works and how it has evolved through the twists and turns of human history. That understanding can help us derive the full benefit of the powers available to us through the Church.

The Nicene Creed was created by the ecumenical Council held at Nicaea in response to a new problem the Church was encountering. Things had gone along fairly well for about 250 years after the Council at Jerusalem, which we read about in the Acts of the Apostles, as the Church handed on in the Gospels and in the Tradition of the Church what Jesus had said and done. Then a priest named Arius, who lived in Alexandria, said, "You know, Jesus is a wonderful person, a wonder worker, a friend of the poor, a great, great teacher, miracle worker even, but he wasn't the Son of God." The bishops answered, "It says in the Scriptures, obviously, that Jesus is the Son of God, is God himself." But Arius said, "No, no, no; you are misunderstanding the

Scriptures. This is what they mean."
And back and forth and back and forth
they went.

Well, the problem the Church faced
at the Council of Nicaea was that this
priest Arius, a clever man, could debate
with the bishops and the pope and
everybody and use Scripture itself as
part of his argument. Scripture by itself
could not solve the problem. Arius
denied the divinity of Christ without
denying any text of Sacred Scripture.
Even today some say all you need is
the Bible, that you do not need the
Sacred Tradition of the Church, the
teachings of the Apostolic fathers which
their successors have handed on from
generation to generation. But Arius and
others like him throughout history
remind us how important it is for us
to know and understand the Sacred
Tradition of the Church which existed
before, gave birth to, and determined
the authenticity of what is called the
canon or list of accepted books of Holy
Scripture. You might even say, to
paraphrase a popular expression, "No
Church, no Bible; know the Church,
know the Bible."

To deal with the problem caused by
Arius, an ecumenical Council of bishops

was called at Nicaea, an ancient city which thrived during Roman times in Asia Minor and today is the Turkish city of Iznik. Bishops are called together at ecumenical Councils because they are the ones the Church has selected and charged with exercising the Apostles' responsibilities and authority. That is why we call bishops "successors of the Apostles." All the bishops of the world who could come to the Council met at Nicaea. Basing their response on Sacred Scripture and the Sacred Tradition of the Church, they refuted Arius. Ever since then, the Church has always held just what we read in the Scriptures and just what we say in the Nicene Creed, that "Jesus is God from God, light from light, true God from true God, begotten not made, one in being with the Father." At the end of that Council, so there would be no more trouble of that sort, all those ancient, wizened, weary bishops said, "Now, from here on out, these are the things you have to believe in order to be a Catholic." That is why we have the Nicene Creed and that is why a practice which continues in both the Western and the Eastern Church — the Latin Church and the Oriental or Eastern Greek Catholic Church — is that every Sunday, year in and year out, we say the Nicene

Creed, except when the Mass contains some other Profession of Faith.

It is easy to see the concerns of the bishops at Nicaea if you compare the two creeds and note the special care taken to preclude misunderstandings that developed in the centuries since the Jerusalem Council. The Apostles' Creed is a very simple one:

"I believe in God, the Father Almighty, Creator of heaven and earth. I believe in Jesus Christ, his only Son, Our Lord. He was conceived by the power of the Holy Spirit and born of the Virgin Mary. He suffered under Pontius Pilate, was crucified, died, and was buried. He descended into hell. On the third day, he rose again. He ascended into heaven and is seated at the right hand of the Father. He will come again to judge the living and the dead. I believe in the Holy Spirit, the holy catholic Church, the communion of saints, the forgiveness of sins, the resurrection of the body, and life everlasting."

Those are the central truths which the Apostles taught following after the example and the teaching of Jesus Christ.

Now, compare that with the Nicene Creed which was created to answer the questions that arose in the 250 years that passed after the Apostles' Creed. The Nicene Creed says:

"We believe in one God, the Father, the Almighty, Maker of heaven and earth, of all that is seen and unseen."

You see, the Apostles' Creed said only, "I believe in God, the Father Almighty, Creator of heaven and earth." In the course of time, however, there were people who said, "Well, maybe God was the Creator of all material things, but what about the spiritual things? Was God only one of several Gods?" And so the Church said, "Maker of heaven and earth, of all that is seen and unseen."

The Apostles' Creed continues, "I believe in Jesus Christ, his only Son, Our Lord." Well, of course, the whole question at issue was, "Who was this Jesus? Was he just a human being or was he also the Son of God?" So the

Council of Nicaea added that we believe in One Lord, "Jesus Christ, the Only Son of God. Eternally begotten of the Father," just so that there should be no doubt. "God from God;" just as the Father is God, the Son is God. "Light from Light;" just as the Father is Light, so is the Son. "True God from True God, begotten not made, One in Being with the Father." Arius and others had said, "Well, Jesus may be the highest of God's creatures, but he is only a creature." "No," the Council said: "Begotten, not made. One in Being with the Father. Through him all things were made. For us men and for our salvation, he came down from heaven" — making explicit the mystery of the Incarnation against those who would say, "No, Jesus was just like Buddha and Confucius and Mahatma Ghandi and all the rest. Wonderful people, wonderful all, but just a man and nothing more."

And then the Council said:

"By the power of the Holy Spirit, he was born of the Virgin Mary and became man. For our sake, he was crucified under Pontius Pilate, he suffered, died and was buried. On the third day, he rose again, in fulfillment of the Scriptures."

Some had said, "Well, Jesus died and was buried and we have his example to remain with us forever, but that's all, just his example." No, the Council said, as Saint Paul clearly pointed out, if Christ is not risen, all of this is in vain. The Resurrection is central, and the Council of Nicaea made explicit that the Resurrection took place in accord with what had been foretold in the Old Testament.

That part of the Nicene Creed concludes with:

> "He ascended into heaven and is seated at the right hand of the Father. He will come again in glory to judge the living and the dead and his kingdom will have no end."

Once that judgment is made, it is eternal.

> Finally we come to the third part of the Apostles' Creed:
> "We believe in the Holy Spirit."

The Council of Nicaea had to add,

> "The Lord, the Giver of Life, who proceeds from the Father and the Son, and with the Father and Son is worshipped and glorified. He has spoken through the Prophets. We believe in one holy, catholic, and apostolic Church."

All the identifying marks of the Church are stated. There are four of them. First, the Church is one. Jesus did not found two, twenty-two hundred, or one hundred and forty-five, but one. Second, the Church is holy, not because we all have halos, but because it is founded by One who is holy and because, in every age and every time and every place, the Church provides for people the means or helps to holiness: the Word of God, the sacraments, the preaching of the Church, the Mass. It is not that everyone in the Church is holy, but that always through time there are holy people in the Church and there is no one who cannot become a saint by using those helps available through the Church. Third, the Church is catholic, which is spelled with a small "c," and means universal or worldwide.

Fourth, the Church is Apostolic, it is founded on the faith of the Apostles and is perpetuated by lines of ordination tracing back to them.

The Nicene Creed ends with,

"We acknowledge one baptism for the forgiveness of sins, we look for the resurrection of the dead and the life of the world to come."

You can see that there are certain common elements found in those two statements of the Church's faith as in others that have been issued through the course of the centuries. That is because creeds address the primary questions that faith in Jesus Christ, in his mission, and in his message entail. Creeds address primary truths. Neither the Apostles' Creed nor the Nicene Creed, for example, mentions angels. Belief in angels is part of our faith, but that belief is not as important as belief in God. We hear talk about, for example, the questions of purgatory or the pains of hell and all those things which are sometimes interesting and sometimes a little scary, but they are theological speculations. They are important, but they are not central parts of the Gospel which Jesus taught. The characteristic note of a creed is always that it does not deal with the secondary or tertiary questions, those that are in second or third place. It deals with the primary elements of the faith that Jesus taught. It deals also with what the purpose of the Church is. The Church is to proclaim the Gospel which enshrines those principal truths. It is to preach the Gospel to every creature as Jesus said just before his Ascension in the Gospel of Saint Matthew.

Teaching those primary, principal truths is the purpose of the creeds and the Councils and all that flows from them. Knowing and living in accordance with those primary, principal truths, we are drawn closer to God and to each other.

There is a story of two brothers who loved each other dearly all their lives. They farmed the land their father had left them jointly and divided its produce share and share alike. One brother married, the other did not. The bachelor brother one day thought to himself, "My share of the profits is far, far more than I need to live on, while my poor brother has a wife and many children to rear." So he began every night to take a sack of grain from his barn and put it in his brother's. Then one day the married brother thought, "I have many children to provide for me in my old age, while my brother has no one. He needs more goods to sell so as to save for his old age." And so he began every night to take a sack of grain from his own barn and put it in his brother's. This went on for a long time, and neither brother could figure out why his store of food did not diminish, until one night they bumped into each other and the truth was out. As they embraced each other, the story goes, the dark night sky became as bright as day and a voice from heaven spoke: "Here at last is the place where I am worshipped in truth. Where brothers meet in love, there am I with them always."

The Church helps us meet in love through its mission of preserving, protecting, defending, and making available to us those primary, principal truths called "the deposit of faith." In that deposit of faith are gracious gifts which, properly conveyed, properly grasped, and properly applied, guide us toward our highest potential — which is love — and the joy of being fully human, fully free, fully alive. In the next chapter, we will explore a valuable tool the Church uses to accomplish that mission.

We live in a world of turmoil but I do not want you to think I am criticizing the world in which we live. It is a good world. It is the world that was given to you and me by God to make better — and the faith of the Church is a very important part of that. The faith is worth knowing and understanding and protecting and putting into practice because it assures you that, in this world of so much turmoil and confusion and conflict, you can have and enjoy the gift of peace. And it is the peaceful person who knows where he or she is going and always goes toward that goal, never away from it. It is the peaceful person who makes a difference, who makes the world better.

A Basic Guide

In the last chapter, you saw that the Nicene Creed provides a much longer statement of the Church's beliefs and teachings than the statement contained in the Apostles' Creed. That is because it was designed to address later attacks directed against the faith of the Church. Safeguarding the faith of the Church against attacks, often by well-meaning, well-intentioned people, is the reason for most of the ecumenical Councils held throughout the long history of our Church. Ecumenical Councils also have been called at times to address new developments and to restate the faith of the Church in terms meaningful to us in each changing age. That was the purpose of the most recent Council, the Second Vatican Council, held at Rome from 1962 to 1965.

Whenever we have had renewal and reform in the Church such as was initiated by the Second Vatican Council, we also have had people who simply did not get it, people who distorted or skewed Council work, and people who became confused and longed for the days when everything seemed clear to them and easier to understand. To address the needs of those who feel they are being tossed about by uncertainty in the wake of the Second Vatican Council, a new *Catechism of the Catholic Church* was published in 1994.

The publication of the catechism was a significant event in the life of the Church because it was the first one completed in more than four hundred years. Its history and that of its predecessors provides us with a kind of brief, summary picture of the whole history of the Church right up to the present age.

In the beginning of the Church, there was no need for what we call a catechism. The number of people entering the Church was, compared to the whole population of the Roman Empire, rather small. It was an underground movement. It was begun in persecution and in secrecy and the Apostles and their successors, the bishops, taught the faith personally to those who were preparing for Baptism, Confirmation, and the first reception of Holy Communion, the Holy Eucharist. Most of the first converts to the Church were adults, so this type of personal instruction could be accomplished for them relatively briefly and simply.

Saint Ambrose, Saint Augustine, and other great teachers in the early Church wrote books which had to do with catechism, but written more from the standpoint of the teacher than the pupil. The word "catechism" comes from a Greek word which means "to drill into," a method by which many have learned the multiplication table or spelling words in grade school. The teacher recites and repeats the material to be learned, then the student repeats it after the teacher, back and forth, back and forth, until the student has it memorized and can apply it.

With the dispersion of the Church throughout the Roman Empire, teaching the faith became more difficult. As long as the people were sharing a common language, a common culture, or at least a common law and a common system of government, communication of information was rather easy. But then the Church began to go into what were called the barbarian lands of France, Spain, Northern Italy, Germany, Austria, Poland, and all the expanse of Europe. The people there could not read and could not understand the languages of Greece and Rome. It became more and more vital that Church teachings be put into simple formulas which the preachers could translate into the languages of the people. Provincial Councils of the Church in the ninth and tenth centuries began urging all bishops to draw up summaries of the faith so that children and those who were not learned could more quickly come to know their faith. That began what we know as the catechetical movement.

The catechetical movement was given further impetus by a great disaster, perhaps the greatest disaster ever suffered by Western Civilization and one we hope will never be repeated, when the Black Death, a form of bubonic plague, reached its height in the years 1347 to 1351. It carried away nearly half the population of Europe. Think of what your community would be if more than 40% of the people living there today would just disappear. That is how the Black Death struck. People who were perfectly well and feeling good at lunch time would be carried off dead of this terrible, terrible disease by dinner time. It turned many cities into ghost towns where all the people were dead or dying and wolves roamed the streets. The plague lasted in its later forms almost down to the foundation of our own country, though in less and less serious epidemics.

Of course, the disease also killed many who attended to the dying. It carried off priests who gave the sacraments to the dying, doctors who were treating them, and lawyers who had to provide them with wills and other instruments for passing on their property. Those were the educated classes of the time, and they were wiped out. Both the Church and the state suffered a severe decline in learning and in culture as a result of the disease. That decline was continued and made worse by the Hundred Years War which lasted at intervals of a hundred successive years from 1337 to 1453. During that time, the countries of Europe were at war and, of course, war takes a terrible toll on children and on knowledge.

In England, at the end of that horrible period, the Archbishop of Canterbury ordered establishment of a system whereby the priests and the deacons were required to teach the Articles of the Creed, the Ten Commandments, the Seven Works of Mercy, the Great Commandment, the Seven Deadly Sins, the Seven Cardinal Virtues, and the Seven Sacraments to the people four times each year. He wrote out the lessons by which they were to teach and thereby created one of the earliest catechisms. An Archbishop of York later provided for the same thing and, on the continent of Europe, the Chancellor of the University of Paris was given the task of providing a French language catechism for use in that nation.

The catechetical movement then was helped along by Martin Luther, a priest of the Augustinian Order who broke away to found his own church. He drew up two catechisms which summarized the teachings he wished to communicate to the people. The catechisms were a great success as instruments for converting people to Lutheranism. When the bishops gathered for the Council of Trent to reassert the teachings of the Church, they chose the catechetical method as the means for teaching the doctrines of the Church to those yet to be converted or to be reconverted to the faith. The catechism which grew out of the Council of Trent was published in two editions, the last of which was in 1571, and it became the norm of teaching in the Church from that day until the catechism published in 1994.

The new catechism follows the same pattern as the catechism published after the Council of Trent. It is divided into four sections. The first section deals with the creed, elaborating and expanding upon the meaning of each article of the creed. The second section deals with the seven sacraments through which we receive the special sacramental graces or gifts of God which initiate us into full communion with his Church, enable us to experience his healing touch in a special way, and empower us to serve him by serving others. The third part of the catechism deals with the life of faith and how we enrich our lives by living in light of the Laws of God expressed in nature and in the Ten Commandments. The fourth part deals with the ultimate purpose of the first three parts — our entering into an ever deepening and expanding relationship with God.

These pages provide you with an introduction to and a sort of companion text for sections of the catechism, but there most certainly is no substitute for the catechism itself — which I heartily commend to you. The catechism is a great gift which Pope John Paul II has given to the Church in our time. It is an authentic and current exposition and summary of what the Church teaches. It is useful as a review of Church teachings for those who may have forgotten important facets first learned long ago. It can be consulted when we are hesitant or doubtful about some particular point of doctrine or of discipline. It is useful in that way, too, as a reference for and as an aid to understanding Scripture. As directed by Pope John Paul II, the new catechism is deeply rooted in Sacred Scripture and every bishop of the Church was consulted in its composition.

It is an authentic source which enables you to check on some of the things that you hear and read about what our Church teaches. As Bishop Fulton Sheen once said, "There is not one person in a thousand who hates what the Church teaches, but there are thousands who hate what they mistakenly believe the Church teaches."

The catechism makes it very simple to know what the Church *really* teaches and to evaluate anything: Catholic periodicals and books, the writings of theologians, sermons and homilies, anything that comes from the persons inside or outside the Church who profess to be accurately presenting or commenting on Church teachings. Does what they say match what the catechism says? If it does, it is correct. If it does not, then it is wrong. The catechism is the antidote for error.

It is meant for all of us. There are those who will say it is a book for teachers only. Not so. They will tell you that the catechism is to be used only by adults, that it is beyond the understanding of any teenager. Not so. The introduction to the catechism expressly tells us it is meant for you and me and for

> "all the faithful who wish to deepen their knowledge of the unfathomable riches of salvation. It is meant to support ecumenical efforts that are moved by the holy desire for the unity of all Christians, showing carefully the content and wondrous harmony of the catholic faith.

The Catechism of the Catholic Church, lastly, is offered to every individual who asks us to give an account of the hope that is in us and who wants to know what the Catholic Church believes."

The new catechism also fosters understanding of other religions in the light of the Catholic faith and is useful for non-Catholics whose religions are traceable to Catholic roots and who want to know more about their early religious heritage. There is among all of us a tendency to think that our religious practice is right and everyone else's is totally and completely wrong, but that is neither right nor healthy. As St. Augustine said and Pope John XXIII often repeated, "In necessary, essential things, we should be one, we should have unity; in non-essential things, we should have diversity; but in all things, everything, each and every thing, we should have charity." So the catechism should be in every Catholic home, not as a weapon to bludgeon people into some sort of mindless conformity, but as a help to ourselves to know and profess our faith and to provide help for others with patience, understanding, and compassion.

It is to draw us closer to God —
and, in so doing, to each other.

In the previous chapter, we dealt with
creeds, which comprise the first section
of the catechism. In the next chapter,
we will begin dealing with sacraments,
the second section of the catechism.

The sacraments are proof that God is constant in his love for us, that he does not abandon us to our own devices, that he always has us in view and takes care of us. He gives us in the sacraments particular helps of grace that we need for the particular times in our lives.

The Economy Of God

The catechism reminds us that our relationships with one another grow directly out of our relationship with God and that everything in the Church is designed to help us realize our highest potential in both — which is love. It does so through what is called "the economy of the Word Incarnate" or "the sacramental economy" or "the economy of salvation."

Some of those terms may be a bit unfamiliar. When we talk about an economy, we generally think of a system for producing and distributing goods. We think of things financial or fiscal or monetary such as the nation's economy or the nation's economic indicators. Each part of the economy — agriculture, mining, manufacturing, technology, and so on — plays a role in meeting our needs for food and clothing and shelter to nurture and sustain life.

The word economy comes from the Greek words "oikos," which means house, and "nemein," which means to manage. They are combined in the Greek word "oikonomia," which is the science of managing a household, of planning and carrying out human life in a home. So we have the terms sacramental economy, economy of the Word, economy of salvation, meaning the plan for what happens in the house of God, in his household of faith. They refer to the way in which God has worked it out, the way in which Christ's Passion, Death, and Resurrection, his Church, his Sacred Scriptures, and his gifts bestowed in the sacraments work together for the good of humankind.

Every household experiences special times and needs — beginnings and endings, separations and reunions, times of joy, times of crisis, times of loss. We come together for weddings, births, deaths, illnesses, graduations, birthdays, anniversaries. Celebrating in joy and consoling in sorrow, the family welcomes, nurtures, strengthens, encourages, and comforts its members. The same is true in the household of faith. The sacramental economy is the way the Church, empowered by and obedient to Christ, welcomes, nurtures, strengthens, encourages, and comforts us in the special times and needs of our lives.

As we consider the sacramental economy, it is important to understand that the sacraments, like so many other things we experience, have a visible and an invisible reality. The visible reality is what our eyes see. When a father or mother hugs his or her child, for example, the visible reality we see is the hug. The invisible reality the hug conveys is love. We cannot "see" the love the hug expresses and conveys, though sometimes we can see its nurturing effect in the child. The visible reality we see in the sacraments is their outward expression, the form they take, the way in which they are administered and received. The invisible reality we cannot "see" is the grace they impart, the power they give us to know and experience and share God's life and love in our lives and the lives of others in a new and deeper way.

Scripture and Sacred Tradition share a common agreement formally confirmed at the Council of Trent, that there are seven sacraments which were instituted by Christ himself to form and nurture his family of faith. For convenience in our understanding of the sacramental economy, we can divide those seven sacraments into three groups. The first are the sacraments of initiation or beginning, sacraments which start us off on our life with Christ. They are Baptism, Confirmation, and Holy Eucharist. The second are the sacraments of healing, the sacraments which help us in our moral or physical weakness. They are the sacrament of Penance or Reconciliation and the sacrament of the Anointing of the Sick. The third are the sacraments of service and vocation which are Holy Orders and Matrimony.

Some may say, "What do you need sacraments for? Jesus and me, that's enough." Of course, if it really is Jesus and not a self-fabricated version of Jesus, and if the one who says it is exempt from normal human needs and frailties, that would be enough. But, Jesus, who is smarter than we are and who has both perfect understanding of and complete compassion for us in our human nature, deemed it necessary to provide the helps the sacraments give us for meeting the trials, challenges, changes, and temptations of life.

Others may say, "I want to go it alone. I want to do it my way." That, of course, is always an option. God forces nothing on us. But we know from what the Church teaches, what our faith believes, and what our experience validates, that no one by himself or herself can please God for long. We need his help. The world, the flesh, and the devil are formidable enemies. True, they cannot conquer you if you do not let yourself be conquered, but they are formidable and they entrap many. If you have any doubt about that, scan the headlines and consider what you read and hear and see: murder, fraud, wars, political corruption of all sorts, child abuse, date rape, addiction, suicide, and on and on — and that does not include our personal failures which go unreported. Almost daily we are reminded how weak we are, how far short we fall of what we might be, how much better we could be in our relationships with each other.

Failures in our human relationships have their root cause in our broken relationship with God. The sacraments are freely offered helps for us which reestablish, confirm, strengthen, renew, and deepen that relationship. Baptism welcomes us into the household of faith and bestows related rights and privileges. Confirmation strengthens us with the living power of God's Holy Spirit. The Eucharist nourishes us on our journey. Penance reconciles us to God and to each other. Matrimony fosters faithful, fruitful, and responsible married love and parenting. Holy Orders confers graces and powers necessary to serve God and his people in the Church. Anointing of the Sick provides healing and comfort in our ailments and in our ultimate passing from this life.

We have the helps we need available to us in the sacraments — but we must do our part to make that help effective in our lives. There is a story about a man who needed help when he was caught in a terrible flood. He climbed a tree and prayed, "Oh Jesus, Jesus, Jesus, save me, save me, save me." A boy in a canoe paddled by and said to the man in the tree, "There's room enough for you in here. Come with me and I'll take you out of here." But the man said, "No thanks, son. You're very kind, but I'm trusting in God. God's going to take care of it." The water kept coming up and up and up and the man began to worry. Then a boat came by and the pilot of the boat pulled over and the people in the boat said, "There's room for you. We'll save you." But the man in the tree said, "No, no, God will save me. I'm waiting for God." They said, "Fine," and went on. Soon the water was up to the man's neck. Just when he could not climb any higher in the tree, a helicopter came by. They dropped a rope and said, "Grab on! We'll take you out of here." But the man said, "No, I'm waiting for God to save me." In a little while, the water went over his head and he drowned. He went to heaven and met God, but he greeted God with a little anger in his voice. He said, "God, I put my trust in you and you did nothing." God answered, "Well, you know, I take care of all my children, and I take care of them well, but what more could I do for you? I sent you a canoe and I sent you a boat and I sent you a helicopter, and you took none of them. I could not help you because you refused all the help I sent. That's why you drowned."

We can refuse the helps the Church offers through the sacraments. We can opt for the "Jesus and me" or "I want to do it my way" course, but that leaves us in the same position as the man in the tree when the flood waters of life threaten.

The sacraments are efficacious helps which draw us closer to God — and to each other — if we are properly prepared and disposed to receive them with the faith which they presuppose, nourish, strengthen, and express. In the next chapter, we will begin to look more closely at the sacraments of initiation and how they are instruments of communion with God and unity among people.

*It is possible to live the life to
which Jesus calls us. It is
possible to win. It is possible to
be faithful and loyal and true
to one another and to God. It
is possible because Jesus Christ
makes it possible. He makes
available to us every help, every
aid, every assistance, every
advantage at every moment of
every day.*

Welcome Home

"Initiation" may seem like a strange term for an expression of love, but that is what each sacrament of initiation is — an expression of unconditional love. The three sacraments of initiation are expressions of love because they are gracious, generous gifts replete with life-changing, life-enriching powers — and they are ours for the asking. They are freely given, not merited or earned by us.

The word initiation comes to us from the Latin "initium," which means beginning, a first step, a start. When most of us think of initiations, we think of familiar rites and rituals which admit us into organizations, societies, clubs, brotherhoods, sisterhoods, fraternities, sororities, and other groups. In each case, our completion of the prescribed initiation brings with it certain rights, privileges, responsibilities, and unity with others.

The sacraments of initiation likewise give us certain rights, privileges, responsibilities, and unity with others. But it is important to remember that they are beginnings only. You could say the powers we receive in the sacraments of initiation are like a baby's muscles at birth. All the muscles are there when the baby is born, but they must be exercised and nourished to grow and develop fully. It is like that with the sacraments. The sacraments of initiation give us powers, but they are not magic. Until we activate and exercise those powers, they remain dormant, latent, dysfunctional.

Baptism, the first sacrament of initiation, is the fundamental, basic, grounding sacrament for the whole Christian faith, the essential sacrament required to start each person off on his or her life with Christ. That is why the catechism describes Baptism as "the gateway to life in the Spirit" and "the door which gives access to the other sacraments."

Baptism is required, but not only because the Church says it is. Baptism is required because Jesus said it is. The Church merely obeys him. There are frequent misunderstandings about Baptism and other sacraments because there are frequent misunderstandings about how the Church works. It is the role of the Church to be obedient and faithful to Jesus Christ, nothing more, nothing less. The Church is obedient and faithful to Christ when it safeguards and passes on to each generation the authentic teachings Jesus entrusted to the Church in its deposit of faith. Baptism is part of that deposit of faith.

Jesus entrusted Baptism to the Church when he told the Apostles gathered with him on the mountain in Galilee, "All power in heaven and on earth has been given to me. Go, therefore, and make disciples of all nations, baptizing them in the name of the Father, and of the Son, and of the Holy Spirit, teaching them to observe all that I have commanded you." You can find that in the Gospel of Saint Matthew, in the 28th chapter, the 18th and 19th verses. In fact, you can find more than 80 references to Baptism in Scripture, including Christ's words to Nicodemus in John 3:5, "No one can enter the kingdom of God without being born of water and Spirit," and his exhortation in the 16th verse of the 16th chapter in the Gospel of Mark, "Whoever believes and is baptized will be saved; whoever does not believe will be condemned."

"Condemned" is a very strong word and can conjure up harsh images of God as a sort of "hanging judge" like the ones we read about in the history of our nation's frontier days. But it is not that way at all. It is as though Jesus finds us wandering cold and wet and hungry, lost in some uncharted wilderness and says, "Please, let me help you. My home is nearby and it's warm and dry and there's food aplenty. I would love to have you come home with me." He issues a gentle invitation, but leaves us free to accept or refuse. Whether we take the shelter offered or continue wandering cold and wet and hungry is our choice. No one sentences or "condemns" us to it.

Because the Church is obligated to be faithful to what Jesus said, there is only one answer it can give to someone who comes to the Church and asks, "How can I have a share in the banquet of life Jesus offers?" The first answer the Church must give is, "Well, if you want a seat at the banquet, you must be baptized." In other words, the door is open, but you have to go through it to get inside. The door is Baptism. Common sense also can help our understanding here. If Jesus has taken the trouble to provide crucial helps for us in the Church and if Baptism is the gateway or door which gives us access to those special helps, then common sense tells us that Baptism is essential.

What about people to whom the Gospel has never come and who have never had the possibility of requesting this sacrament? Does this mean that God just cuts them off? Does God just say to them, "Too bad, the missionary made it to the station before yours, but he got off the train there and so you didn't get it. Too bad." Is that how we view God? No. God sometimes instructs us as you instruct a child — simply. You tell a child, "Look both ways before you cross a street." You do not try to describe for the child every possible hypothetical situation that could occur or call attention to low flying objects or the danger of earthquakes or lightning striking the telephone pole on the other side of the street and so on. No, you just say, "Look both ways before you cross a street." All the contingencies will take care of themselves as the child grows older. In the same way, God instructs us. "Look, if you want what I have to offer, be baptized." With regard to all those situations and contingencies which involve others, God says to us equivalently, "You let me worry about that. You concentrate on getting your own act together. Let me run the world."

His instructions to the Church are equally focused: "Go into the whole world. Proclaim the good news. Baptize." That is what the Church must do. In obeying, the Church is limited in its scope and authority. God, however, is not. We do not know exactly how God views the economy of salvation in its broadest context. Those questions are in limbo. Limbo is an Italian word which comes from the Latin word "limbus" and means margin. Early books were printed with very wide margins because of the way paper was made and printing was done. People in the Middle Ages and later Middle Ages wrote notes in those margins. When something was not covered in the text of Scripture, theologians would write questions in the margin, "in limbo." We can speculate about those questions, but we only know what we were given by Revelation and reminded of by the Second Vatican Council: "Since Christ died for all and since all are in fact called to one and the same destiny which is divine, we must hold that the Holy Spirit offers to all the possibility of being made partakers (in God's saving plan) in a way known to God." It is not the role of the Church to determine the exact nature and exact workings of God's relationship with each man, woman, and child living in every imaginable circumstance and situation. It is the role of the Church to be an obedient and faithful expression of and effective instrument for God's love in the world.

Why does Christ prescribe Baptism with words and water? That is a question you will have to ask him when you see him. Maybe it was to make it easier for us. He could have required that we get a doctor of divinity degree from some ancient university or make pilgrimages and collect coupons or climb to the top of some remote mountain and sign a list, but he chose instead to make it easily available to everyone who asks.

Baptism's easy availability and the gifts it provides are reminiscent of the Gospel story of the prodigal son. The wayward son in the story left home and squandered his inheritance. He finally realized in the midst of the misery he created for himself that he had made a horrible, horrible mistake. Hoping his father would take him back as a hired hand, he started for home. He had no idea how much his father loved him and wanted him back. Scripture tells us, "While he was still a long way off, his father caught sight of him, and was filled with compassion. He ran to his son, embraced him, and kissed him." His father did not even wait for him to finish his apology. He welcomed him home and showered him with gifts: the finest robe, a ring, sandals, and a great celebration. Baptism is like that.

Baptism deals with what might be called our squandered inheritance and the reaction of a Father who loves us far more than we can imagine. The squandered inheritance I refer to is traceable to the first chapters of the Book of Genesis and the story of Adam and Eve. We are told God and they were friends, but they chose to reject that relationship with God, a rejection which had consequences for them and for us. In that respect, you could say we are like the Stuart offspring in Europe. Wandering around on the European landscape somewhere today are people who are members of the

Stuart family, and one of them would be the king of England right now, except that his ancestor, King James II, abdicated the throne in 1688. He just quit, left, ran away. He spent the rest of his life in exile, and the crown ultimately passed out of the Stuart family. Had King James stayed, his descendants would be the royal family today while Elizabeth's offspring, Prince Charles, Prince William, and their crowd would be speaking German back in Hanover where they were spawned. Today the Stuarts are born into the condition of non-royalty, not because of any fault of their own, but because of the fault of their ancestor.

The point of the story in Genesis is that we are not what we could be because we, like the Stuarts, lost our inheritance. We lack something God intended to give us. Our lost inheritance is a consequence of what is sometimes called "original sin," a term often misunderstood. We tend to think of original in the sense of the Original Amateur Hour, the first one, or the original Orville Redenbacher popcorn, meaning not an imitation. But in the term original sin, original means from our origin, the sin of origin.

Sin is a term used to describe a particular kind of human folly or foolishness, a dullness of mind and spirit which clouds our understanding and makes us lose sight of life's meaning and purpose. It is our defiance of God or our transgression of God's laws. Sin is folly because it makes no sense to defy someone whose only attitude toward us is complete and perfect love. It is folly because it makes no sense to transgress laws which safeguard our own happiness. The human folly or foolishness which we call sin is of two kinds. The first is original sin, the one we just traced back to our origin. The second kind is called "actual sin," another term often misunderstood. We think of actual as meaning real, something which actually happened. In the term actual sin, it means from our acts, from our own actions.

Misunderstandings about what sin is and about what the difference is between original sin and actual sin have led to some misguided attacks on the Church regarding the baptizing of children. You may hear someone say, "How can a little baby have a sin on its innocent soul? And how can those terrible Catholics say they have to have a sacrament to take it away from an innocent little baby?" That kind of comment is crass ignorance, the worst kind of ignorance. All of us are guilty of ignorance to some extent. We may not be able to sing the Star Spangled Banner in Chinese, for example. That is ignorance, but not crass ignorance. It is an ignorance most Americans share because there is no necessity for us to know the Chinese language if we are not going to be in China or work in a field which uses that language. Are you ignorant of Chinese? Yes. Can you attribute that to yourself as a fault? No. Crass ignorance is the kind that is a fault. In America, not knowing a red, octagonal traffic sign means "stop" is crass ignorance. If you are a driver — or a pedestrian — and you do not know that, you are a danger to yourself and others. It is something you should know. Some things which are said about the Church and about the sacraments constitute crass ignorance. Those who talk about the Church and its teachings have a responsibility in justice, in basic human decency, and as an act of elementary human intelligence to first find out from the authentic, legitimate Church authority, from the Magisterium, what the truth is.

The truth is that the sacrament of

Baptism is the restoration of our inheritance or birthright. It is the equivalent of the father in the story of the prodigal son rushing out to greet us and showering gifts upon us, the gifts we lack but our Father intended us to have. It is our Father embracing us and welcoming us home again with a happy celebration.

The only really creative force in the universe is the power of love. It is a mighty power. And if you exercise it with faith in God, it can help you overcome every obstacle in your life.

Hope For The Future

As if the warm welcoming and restoration of our birthright with the gifts bestowed in Baptism were not enough, we are showered with more gifts in the second sacrament of initiation, which is called Confirmation. The word Confirmation comes to us from the Latin term "firmare," which means to strengthen. You can read about Confirmation and the theology of the Holy Spirit in the Gospel of Saint John, chapters 14, 15, and 16. It was foretold when Jesus said, "The Advocate, the Holy Spirit that the Father will send in my name — he will teach you everything and remind you of all that I have told you." And again, in Acts of the Apostles, chapters 1 and 2, we see described the effect of Confirmation in emboldening us and in making us witnesses for Christ to others as the gifts which we receive in Baptism are confirmed or strengthened.

Among the gifts received in Baptism and strengthened in Confirmation are:

- The gift of faith, not just the kind of faith we place in the surgeon who operates on us or the pilot who guides our flight, but the theological virtue of faith. The catechism describes that faith as the power which enables us "to believe in God, to hope in him, and to love him."

- The gift of hope, not just the kind of hope we have for good weather when we plan a cookout or head for the beach, but the theological virtue of hope. The catechism describes that hope as the power which enables us to have union with God as our primary goal in life, "placing our trust in Christ's promises and relying not on our own strength, but on the helping grace of the Holy Spirit."

- The gift of love, not just the kind of love we have for parents and children and spouses and friends and pets, but the theological virtue of love which often is referred to as "charity." The catechism describes that love or charity as the power which enables us to "love God above all things for his own sake, and our neighbor as ourselves for the love of God."

By bestowing those gifts — the theological virtues of faith, hope, and love — the sacrament of Baptism restores us to a right relationship with God, which opens us to a right relationship with each other and with nature. It gives us a fresh start, a clean slate, a new beginning, free of the baggage and burdens of original sin and, for those baptized as adults, actual sin occurring before Baptism. It gives us membership in the family of Christ, called the Mystical Body or the People of God, and provides access to all the powers Christ makes available to his family through the Church. All of those gifts are given to us in the sacrament of Baptism and are strengthened in Confirmation.

Why did Christ include Confirmation in the Church's deposit of faith? That, too, is a question you will have to ask him when you see him. Maybe it had something to do with our need for strength to meet the challenges he knew we would meet living in a world that is indifferent or hostile to him. Since not everyone is baptized, renewed, restored, and since some who are baptized do not actively exercise their baptismal powers, the world we live in remains subject to the consequences of the sin of origin, the original rejection of God. Some still reject God and, repeating the folly of Genesis, prefer to do things their own way. As a result, there is disorder in our world and we remain subject to all the temporal consequences of sin outlined in the catechism: suffering, illness, addictions, death, weaknesses of character, a tendency to misuse God's beautiful creation, and an inclination toward the ugliness we see in what are called the capital sins: greed, lust, anger, gluttony, pride, envy, and sloth.

It is not difficult for any thinking person to grasp the concept of original sin and our need for help and strength to deal with it if he or she simply reads or hears and watches the daily news.

As others have observed, daily news reports make it easier to understand original sin and hell than to understand our redemption and heaven. But the powers of faith and hope and love given us in Baptism and strengthened in Confirmation safeguard us from that cynical outlook. The news of the day may cause some to look around and say, "What can I do? Nothing." But Jesus tells us, "No, not quite. Fear not. Fear not. I have overcome the world. I have overcome all this. Stick with me and you'll make it. And not only will you make it yourself — because just looking out for yourself is not the aim of a faithful Catholic Christian; a faithful Catholic Christian does not think like that. No, you also will make a difference. Making a difference is making someone else's life better. And you can do that if you have faith."

Where do we get that kind of faith, the theological virtue of faith? We get it with our Baptism. We increase it by exercising it and by drawing on that rich deposit of faith available to us in the Church: the sacraments, Sacred Scripture, and Tradition. Failing to draw on that rich deposit of faith is like having millions of dollars in the bank, but choosing to live a life impoverished and forlorn. Sadly, that is just what some choose for themselves in their spiritual lives, even some who know about the Church and its sacraments. Knowing *about* the Church and its sacraments is never enough. That would reduce all this to a mere intellectual exercise, like a classroom lecture we hear and forget the moment we exit. Our hope for the future begins to be realized when those sacramental powers are made active, made incarnate, in us.

Baptism is the beginning. Activation and renewal and increase of the powers with which we were graced in Baptism are ours for the asking. Simply pray:

Father Creator, Jesus Redeemer, Holy Spirit Sanctifier: renew and increase in me your gifts of faith, hope, and love; faith, that I may believe as you would have me believe; hope, that I may keep you first and foremost in my life and that I may trust in your gifts to guide and strengthen me; love, that I may show my faith and hope in action by my respect and care for you and my respect and care for all others.

In the next chapter, we will explore additional gifts bestowed in the sacraments of initiation, gifts which help us live up to our full potential, our full dignity, fully human, fully free, and fully alive.

If you really wish to be a productive and happy member of this society, you will need with absolute necessity the help of God given to you in the seven Gifts of the Holy Spirit. All of them are necessary for a happy life.

Habits Of Love

Earlier I asked you to consider: do you think that if everyone on earth, all six billion people, kept the Ten Commandments, do you think this would be a worse world or a better one? The answer is obvious when you imagine a world of justice and peace; a world without lying, cheating, and stealing; without murder and rape and adultery; without pollution and corruption and exploitation. What you are picturing is the world as God intended it to be, the world we are empowered to restore with the gifts bestowed in Baptism and strengthened in Confirmation.

Those powers and the virtues or habits which flow out of them are living, vital, dynamic forces with power to reshape us and the world around us. They enrich our lives with what St.

Paul calls "the fruit of the Spirit" —
signs or effects of the powers of Baptism
and Confirmation at work in us. The
catechism cites twelve of those signs
or effects, qualities which come into
our lives when we exercise the powers
of Baptism and Confirmation:

—Love,
—Joy,
—Peace,
—Patience,
—Kindness,
—Goodness,
—Generosity,
—Faithfulness,
—Modesty,
—Gentleness,
—Self-Control, and
—Chastity.

Lives filled with those qualities — not
strife and fear and discord — are our
birthright, the inheritance originally
intended for us by our Father. They
are ours when we are living lives worthy
of men and women and children made
in the image and likeness of God.

Anything less is beneath our dignity,
like the condition Bishop Sheen once
described. "When we see a worm
crawling in the mud," he said, "it does

not disturb us. That is the worm's destiny. It was made to crawl in the mud. But when we see a beautiful bird dragging a broken wing through the mud, it tears at our hearts. It tears at our hearts because we know the bird was made for greater things, a higher destiny." And so it is with us. We are not made to crawl in the mud of materialism and moral decay. We are made for greater things, a higher destiny. And those greater things, that higher destiny — communion with God and unity with each other — are what the Church and its sacraments help us attain.

The powers bestowed in Baptism and strengthened in Confirmation — faith, hope, and love — are the beginning. To counter tendencies toward the folly and foolishness of sin, to fortify us against this world's subtle enticements and its powerful temptations to corruption, and to strengthen us through the normal trials of living in a less than perfect world, Baptism also bestows and Confirmation enhances what are called the seven Gifts of the Holy Spirit. Those Gifts or powers begin restoration of the inheritance our Father intended for us. Just as the sin of origin, the original rejection of God, left us with tendencies toward the ugliness so well documented in the daily news, the seven Gifts of the Holy Spirit give us the power to replace those tendencies with tendencies or dispositions to do good.

All validly baptized men, women, and children are graced with those seven Gifts of the Holy Spirit — Wisdom, Understanding, Counsel, Fortitude, Knowledge, Piety, and Reverence.

1. Wisdom

Wisdom, the first Gift, is the ability to use our acquired knowledge and learning for its right purpose, the purpose for which God intends within the order of the universe. Without Wisdom, knowledge goes awry. We misuse our knowledge and pollute our atmosphere or create mighty engines of destruction. Virtually all evil results from misusing knowledge originally meant to be used for our good. Today we have more acquired knowledge than any other people ever has enjoyed in the history of humankind, but lack of Wisdom often deprives us of the benefits and joy which our knowledge, rightly used, could and should provide us.

2. Understanding

Understanding, the second Gift, is the ability to comprehend what we have accepted in faith. It takes us beyond vague, child-like belief and enables us to see the meaning and purpose of what has been revealed to us. Without Understanding, religion can become superstition. You could say faith is like acknowledging that airplanes can fly; Understanding is like grasping the principles of aerodynamics which make them fly.

3. Counsel

Counsel, the third Gift, is the ability to know the right thing to do, the prudent thing to do, in the various situations we encounter. You could say it enables us to hear God speaking to us and guiding us, telling us what we should do — and what we should avoid. Without Counsel, we are like visitors traveling at night in a strange land with no guide, no map, no compass, and no light to help us find our way. Counsel helps us know and see where we are going, guides us past the pitfalls and dead-ends of bad choices, and helps us realize our full potential.

4. Fortitude

Fortitude or courage, the fourth Gift, is the ability to persevere in doing what we know is right, in doing what we know is the truly loving thing to do despite personal setbacks and losses. It is the power to carry on despite inconvenience, fatigue, discomfort, or disappointment; to persist in doing right despite unpopularity, criticism, ridicule, or persecution. Fortitude enables us to endure hardships out of love for and faithfulness to God and strengthens us in our trials as Christ was strengthened at Gethsemane. Without the Gift of Fortitude, we are like power tools running weakly on exhausted batteries instead of performing full strength on AC current.

5. Knowledge

Knowledge, the fifth Gift, is the ability to see our lives and the world from a spiritual perspective instead of the merely physical and material. The Gift of Knowledge is different from the kind of knowledge or learning we acquire through study and experience. It is the gift which enables us to see our lives and the world "through the eyes of God," with all its beauty and order leading us to love of and union with

God and each other — as was originally intended. Without the Gift of Knowledge, our vision is distorted and we have trouble distinguishing between good and evil, between inspiration and temptation.

6. Piety

Piety or love, the sixth Gift, is the ability to see God as a loving Father whose only concern is for our ultimate happiness. It instills in us a sense of his overwhelmingly incomprehensible love for you and for me and for all of his creation. Piety enables us to approach God, his Church, his teachings, his commandments, his Sacred Scriptures, and his sacraments, with affection, respect, and loyalty. Without Piety, we tend to see God as an insensitive, legalistic taskmaster out to control and manipulate and flog us — and we tend to see his Church the same way. Piety fills us with a joyful sense of God's compassion for us manifest in Christ and the Church and moves us to share that compassion with others.

7. Reverence

Reverence, the seventh Gift, is the ability to see God as God. It enables us to have a distinct, intense, humbling awareness of his greatness, his majesty, his power, and his transcendence. The Gift of Reverence sometimes is referred to as "fear of the Lord," but many misunderstand that to mean the fear a slave might have for a cruel master. On the contrary, "fear of the Lord" is the kind of fear we have of hurting or offending someone we love very much, someone who is both very important to us and very kind to us. Without the Gift of Reverence, we tend to think of God as distant and indifferent, like someone we have heard of or have seen on TV, but never met. With the Gift of Reverence, we live in a deeply felt relationship with God, aware of his presence and power, and aware that all others and all creation are his.

Though all validly baptized men, women, and children are graced with those seven Gifts, not all validly baptized men, women, and children are fruitfully baptized. You could say that being validly baptized is like being given a valid library card. The card gives you the right and the power to check out books and other items, but the card is fruitless, is of no benefit to you, unless and until you decide to use it. It is similar to that with the gifts we receive at Baptism. We can use them, ignore them, even throw them away. Though Baptism is the restoration of our original relationship with God, a relationship of love, it forces nothing on us. We always remain free to reject both the gifts and the Giver. That is because Baptism, like the other sacraments, is an expression of love, a freely bestowed gift, an invitation to love — and the essence of love is that it cannot be forced or coerced. We cannot love unless we are free not to love.

The Gifts of the Holy Spirit enable us to become better lovers — if we choose to. They help us form habits of love, habits which are called moral virtues. The catechism cites and describes the effects of four principal or cardinal virtues which help us "govern our actions, order our passions, and guide our conduct according to reason and faith. They make possible ease, self-mastery, and joy in leading a morally good life." The four principal or cardinal virtues are prudence, justice, temperance, and fortitude.

- Prudence is the habit of focusing on the true good in every circumstance and of choosing the right means to achieve the true good.

- Justice is the habit of respecting the rights of God and of all others in every circumstance.

- Temperance is the habit of mastering our instincts and keeping our desires within the limits of what is honorable in every circumstance.

- Fortitude is the habit of constantly pursuing what is good in every circumstance despite facing difficulties and temptations and obstacles.

Those habits of love — or moral virtues — make us better lovers because they bring out the best in us — the God in us. They make it easier for us to do what is right and avoid what is wrong. That is something about the moral life many people miss — that acting rightly is just as much a habit as acting wrongly, that we form and strengthen good habits which make it easier for us to do what is right and avoid what is wrong in the very same way we form harmful habits.

That is why we need never despair or grow cynical. Through the sacraments of initiation, we enter into a unity with God and with each other which means we never have to go it alone. It is as though Jesus comes to us and says, "Look, I know you better than you know yourselves. I know what's in your hearts, what it's like to be human, and I'm here to help. Trust me. I won't change your nature and take away your free will or turn you into a holy robot. What I will do is make some helps available for you. You decide whether to use them. No matter what you do, I love you. There is nothing you can do to make me stop loving you."

As if to prove his love, he proceeds to give us the third sacrament of initiation, the Eucharist, often called the Most Blessed Sacrament. In the next chapter, we will explore why it is called that and why the catechism calls it "the source and summit" of all our spiritual life.

The world spends most of its time trying to make God in the image and likeness of man, as though driven by some infernal instinct to cut God down to size. That has two results: first, God won't have it; second, it gives us a very distorted notion of God.

Love Without Limit

Eucharist, the third sacrament of initiation, also is known by many other names — for good reason: each name captures an aspect of the sacrament, but none can capture the totality.

Let me explain why. There is an old story about the leader of a primitive inland tribe who had never traveled more than a few miles from his prairie home and had never seen a body of water larger than a small lake. A trusted government agent took him across the plains and over the mountains to show him the ocean. As he approached the sea, the prairie dweller was awestruck. The endless expanse of blue-green water; the roar of enormous waves topped by whitecaps crashing against jagged, sea-worn rocks with an explosion of spray; the seemingly motionless gulls riding the wind and hovering overhead; the wind-borne sand and saltwater mist, all presented themselves to him in a cavalcade of wonders. He stood transfixed, marveling at everything before him. After a while, he waded into the waves and dipped an empty jar into the water. As he put the lid on the jar and returned to shore, he explained that he wanted to take it back to his people on the prairie so they could see the ocean, too.

Our best efforts to describe the Eucharist are like that tribal leader's effort to show his people the ocean in a small jar of still water. Even the most descriptive terms by which the Eucharist is known afford us only a faint hint of its majesty, its beauty, its power to change us — and the limitless love behind it.

That limitless love and its power to change us are why the catechism refers to the Eucharist as "the Sacrament of sacraments" and "the sum and summary of our faith." All of the other sacraments and all of the teachings and works of the Church flow from and are strengthened by the Eucharist.

The word Eucharist comes to us from the Greek words "eucharistia" and "eucharistos" which mean grateful, thankful. The term Eucharist is used for the third sacrament of initiation because it was during the prayer of thanksgiving at the Last Supper that Jesus entrusted this sacrament to the Church. Saint Paul describes it for us in chapter 11 of the first letter to the Corinthians: "The Lord Jesus, on the night he was handed over, took bread, and, after he had given thanks, broke it and said, 'This is my body that is for you. Do this in remembrance of me.' In the same way also the cup, after supper, saying, 'This cup is the new covenant in my blood. Do this, as often as you drink it, in remembrance of me.' For as often as you eat this bread and drink the cup, you proclaim the death of the Lord until he comes."

Then, as if to emphasize that it is not mere symbolic bread and wine of which he speaks, Paul warns, "Whoever eats the bread or drinks the cup of the Lord unworthily will have to answer for the body and blood of the Lord." In those words, Paul pointedly echoes the Eucharistic teaching of Christ set forth in the Gospels of Matthew, Mark, and Luke; accentuated in the Gospel of John; affirmed in the Epistles and Acts; upheld since the time of Christ by the

Church, and expressed explicitly in such terms for the Eucharist as "the Body and Blood of Christ" and "the Real Presence."

The Real Presence of Christ in the Eucharist has been a sort of litmus test of faith for followers of Jesus since the time Christ first spoke of it. Three common stumbling blocks hinder understanding of this central sacrament: first, some claim Jesus did not mean what he said; second, some think having Christ truly present in the Eucharist is impossible, and third, some cannot understand *why* God would choose to remain with us in the form of bread and wine.

The first stumbling block is addressed most directly by Jesus in the sixth chapter of the Gospel of John. After Jesus had said that he was the bread of life, his followers started murmuring to each other about his strange talk. But then, instead of backing down or softening his words, Jesus responded even more forcefully: "I am the bread of life. Your ancestors ate the manna in the desert, but they died; this is the bread that comes down from heaven so that one may eat it and not die. I am the living bread that came down from heaven; whoever eats this bread will live forever; and the bread that I will give is my flesh for the life of the world."

And what happens next? His followers start arguing among themselves. "How can this man give us his flesh to eat?" Again Jesus answers, this time still more strongly: "Unless you eat the flesh of the Son of Man and drink his blood, you do not have life within you. Whoever eats my flesh and drinks my blood has eternal life, and I will raise him on the last day. For my flesh is true food, and my blood is true drink. Whoever eats my flesh and drinks my blood remains in me and I in him."

As if to make any misunderstanding absolutely impossible, Jesus uses here a particularly strong word for eat which means "to bite off and chew." Likewise, the word he uses for flesh is not the more polite equivalent of our word "meat," but the harsher word "flesh." Many of his followers found those words intolerable and asked how anyone could accept it. Again Jesus stood resolute: "For this reason I have told you that no one can come to me unless it is granted him by my Father." Saint John goes on to say, "As a result of this, many of his disciples returned to their former way of life and no longer accompanied him." They understood exactly what he was saying, and they knew Jesus meant what he said.

What is important to note here is what Jesus did *not* say to those who turned and walked away. He did not say, "Wait. Come back. Maybe you misunderstood. Let's talk about it." He did not say that. He said nothing to them. In fact, Saint John says, Jesus then turned to the Apostles, the twelve, and asked, "Do you also want to leave?" Jesus meant what he said.

Some have turned and walked away from the Eucharist, the Body and Blood of Christ, the Real Presence, in every age, despite Christ's cautioning that it is pivotal, central, vital, crucial to growth in our relationship with him and, therefore, with each other. From the very beginning, there have been those who sought to divide the Church by attacking what the catechism describes as our "sign of unity," and "bond of charity." In the first century, it was the Gnostics; in the second century, the Docetists; in the third century, the Manacheans, and so on right up to the Reformation in the Middle Ages when most, though not all, who turned away from the Church began by turning away from the Eucharist. Through all those ages, from the Fathers of the Church, those who knew Christ, who knew the Apostles, Saint John Chrysostom, Saint Cyril, Saint Justin Martyr, Saint Augustine, and all the rest, through the Councils, including the Council of Trent which responded to the Reformation with the reaffirmation that Jesus is "truly, really, and substantially" present in the Eucharist, the Church has, as with one voice, proclaimed that Jesus said what he meant and meant what he said: "Take and eat. This is my body. Take and drink. This is my blood."

The second stumbling block for some is the belief that such a thing is impossible. Well, that depends on how you think of God and who you think Jesus is. A recent Gallup poll reported that 96 percent of Americans see God as the ultimate source of our material and spiritual world. Of course, there are all kinds of theories about God, most of which leave us in the untenable position of trying to understand an Infinite Being with a finite mind — which is like trying to pour a gallon of milk into a quart bottle. Most of those ideas and theories restrict God to doing only what we decree is possible and permissible, which imprisons God within the narrow confines of our limited understanding and imagination. That pathetic condition calls to mind what a knowledgeable listener said after hearing an atheist friend's pitiful, childish description of God: "I don't believe in the god you don't believe in, either."

I AM WHO AM, the God of Abraham, Isaac, and Jacob, the God of the Old Testament and the New Testament, the God who seeks to draw us to himself and to each other through the gifts of life and love he gives us in the Church, does not ask for our permission to act or not to act, does not restrict himself to behavior we always understand, and certainly is not predictable. On the contrary, salvation history, the history of God's relationship with humankind, would suggest that the only thing predictable about God is unpredictability. The prophet Isaiah affirms that: "For my thoughts are not your thoughts, nor are your ways my ways, says the Lord. As high as the heavens are above the earth, so high are my ways above your ways and my thoughts above your thoughts." (Isa. 55:8-9)

In fact, unpredictability and showing up in ways we least expect seem to be a constant pattern in God's relationship with us. When the prophet Elijah, in the first book of Kings, is told, "Go outside and stand on the mountain before the Lord; the Lord will be passing by," we naturally anticipate a display of power and might. But, we are told, "A strong and heavy wind was rending the mountains and crushing rocks before the Lord — but the Lord was not in the wind. After the wind, there was an earthquake — but the Lord was not in the earthquake. After the earthquake, there was fire — but the Lord was not in the fire. After the fire, there was a tiny whispering sound . . ." — and there, where we would least expect, was the Lord. (1Kgs. 19:11-13)

So it is with the Eucharist. It is as if the Lord delights in short-circuiting our logical, analytical minds and in repeatedly teaching us to expect the unexpected. Who could expect or predict that God would select a small nomadic tribe to be his chosen people? That he would speak through a burning bush or use "a column of cloud by day and a column of fire by night" to lead his chosen people out of slavery? That he would promise a Savior and foretell his coming through more than a dozen prophets, yet the Savior would be recognized by only a handful of people? That the Savior would be born in a stable under apparently suspicious circumstances and be known as the son of a Jewish carpenter? That the very people to whom his coming was foretold would scorn and taunt him as a heretic and traitor? That he would be content with a motley crew of 12 slowwitted Apostles, one of whom would betray him and all of whom would abandon him in crisis? That he would be subjected to heinous torture, be crucified, and be raised from the dead? That out of those fickle and cowardly first Apostles he would build a Church encompassing the world, courageously surviving countless internal clashes and external attacks, and enduring through the rise and fall of civilization after civilization? In light of all that, it should be clear to any observer — certainly clear to the 82% of Americans whom the Gallup poll identifies as Christians, one third of whom are Catholic — that it not only is possible, but is perfectly consistent for him to stay with us, "truly, really, and substantially" present in the Eucharist under the appearances of bread and wine — where we would least expect.

The third stumbling block for some is understanding *why* God would choose to remain with us in the form of bread and wine. There is an old story from way back, eight or nine hundred years ago, when a King of England known as Richard the Lionhearted was leading the Crusades, a military effort to recover the Holy Land from the followers of the prophet Mohammed. King Richard was captured by the Moslems and was put up, not in prison, but as the guest of Saladin, the Moslem sultan or ruler. Richard and Saladin became friends and talked about everything, explaining and sharing an understanding of each other's religion. On one occasion, the sultan said to Richard, "You know, your religion, Christianity, has many, many beautiful things in it. But," he said, "it fails to recognize the majesty of God. You believe that the Son of God becomes a piece of bread. That is beneath the dignity of God." Richard replied, "Well, your majesty, your religion, the religion of Mohammed, has many beautiful things in it, too. But," he said, "it fails to recognize the love of God. So much does God love us that he wishes to be with us always, in good times and in bad, to remain among us in the Holy Sacrament of the Altar, and to be our food during life's difficult journey." The

Moslem scribe who wrote all this down says, "And the sultan thereafter was silent."

The sultan was silent because he and the king were face to face with what Pope John Paul II, in his first encyclical letter, "Redemptor Hominis," calls "the ineffable sacrament," the sacrament for which words are inadequate because we are "incapable of grasping and translating into words what the Eucharist is in all its fullness, what is expressed by it, and what is actuated by it." Words fail us because love can never be fully expressed in words, and the Eucharist is God's greatest, highest expression of love — his unconditional, infinite love for us. Words fail us because love transcends words. To see what I mean, go to an arrival gate at an airport and watch how loved ones greet each other after a long separation. They cry; they laugh; they hug; they can hardly speak in their exuberance, so intense is their joy. Words come later. And so it is with all of us in our deeply moving moments of love.

You could say the Eucharist, the supreme moment of love, shows a sort of divine exuberance for you and me. Many of us have a hard time accepting that because we have a hard time understanding that each one of us — with all our flaws and faults and failings — is, in the eyes of God, completely beautiful, precious beyond price, and loved beyond words. Many of us have a very hard time accepting that because we underestimate our real worth. We underestimate our real worth because we cannot understand our real worth without understanding the death of Christ. And we cannot understand the death of Christ without understanding the life of Christ.

The life of Christ is not the story of someone who was caught running away. At the beginning of John's Gospel, we are told, "And the Word became flesh and dwelt among us." In Hebrew, those words mean he "pitched his tent among us." In other words, Jesus wanted to be here, chose to be here, with the likes of you and me. It was as though Jesus said, "I like those people. I love them. I'd like to be with them." And so "the Word became flesh and dwelt among us."

Jesus could have worked out our redemption in a thousand, thousand myriad ways, of course, but this is the way he chose. He chose to become one of us, to live among us, to take on the burden we carry in the wake of our lost inheritance, and to experience life as we experience it. That is what Saint Paul means in his letter to the Phillippians: "He emptied himself, taking the form of a slave, coming in human likeness; and found human in appearance, he humbled himself, becoming obedient to death, even death on a cross." Why? Because he had no choice? No. "He took on the form" — it was not forced on him. "He humbled himself, becoming obedient to death" — it was not forced on him. He did all that because he chose to do it. He chose it because he thought you and I were worth it. He thought you and I were worth it because he loves us.

So what are we worth? It depends on whose answer you decide to accept. Materialists say we are made of chemicals worth less than $10. Some politicians say we are worth whatever we contribute to the state, which was the Nazi rationale for killing "nonproductive eaters." Hollywood says our worth is determined by our fame and looks. Wall Street says we are worth whatever we buy and own. Madison Avenue says we are worth whatever styles we wear or drive. The Church, which is hated by some because it stands, often alone, against all the degrading, demoralizing, dehumanizing forces which reduce men, women, and children to mere things or economic units, says our value is infinite. The Church says our value is infinite because we — everyone, each one of us, from womb to tomb, regardless of ability or disability, regardless of race, religion, gender, age, ethnic group, political views, and all the other categories some use to divide us — all of us have been redeemed, purchased, ransomed for a price. That price is the life and death of Jesus Christ. And that is why, in the eyes of God, we are precious beyond price and loved beyond words.

Remember that. That is the essence of the Eucharist, the essence of our faith, the foundation of human dignity, and the reason the Church exists. If you forget all the rest of the trappings of religion, if you forget all the dogmas and all the doctrines and all the commandments, remember that. When we have Jesus in the Eucharist, the Most Blessed Sacrament, we have Jesus, not where we want him, but where he wants us — together in hope, united in faith, strengthened in love.

The Eucharist is Jesus, uniting us to himself, uniting us to one another, and bringing us back from the despair so many feel so deeply today.

"Happy Are Those . . ."

Because in the Eucharist we are being brought together in hope, united in faith, strengthened in love, redeemed, empowered, and nourished, we have good reason for confidence and joy, even in our most trying times. We are reminded of that at each Eucharistic celebration — called the "Holy Sacrifice of the Mass" — when the priest who consecrates the bread and wine raises the host just before communion and says, "This is the Lamb of God who takes away the sins of the world. Happy are those who are called to his supper."

At first glance it may seem strange to see the words "celebration" and "happy" used in connection with a sacrifice, particularly the sacrifice of Jesus on the cross. That is because the spirit of sacrifice is misunderstood by and is contrary to the spirit of this passing age. Some elements of American society — caught in the grip of secularism and materialism — fear, shun, reject, and run away from any mention of sacrifice or suffering. Yet the spirit of sacrifice is a central element in both our national and spiritual heritage and is essential to true human love; where there is no spirit of sacrifice, there is no authentic love.

We often hear the word "sacrifice" used to describe sufferings like those our nation's founders endured: five who signed their names to our Declaration of Independence were taken captive as traitors and tortured; twelve had their homes looted and burned; two lost sons in the battles which followed; nine fought and died themselves from wounds or hardship. Our history is replete with men and women and children, too, who sacrificed their own comfort and even their lives for the liberty of others. The aura of deep respect we often find at national cemeteries and monuments honoring them is a measure of our esteem and gratitude. You could say that national holidays such as our annual Fourth of July observances are happy celebrations of their sacrifices which set us free. Our Eucharistic celebration has similar aspects, but is far more profound, both in substance and in effect. It is the celebration of a sacrifice which set us free, but is not a mere anniversary observance. It is the celebration of an event which not only happened, but which is continuing to happen at this very moment, a sacrifice which not only set us free, but which sustains and nourishes our spiritual freedom each time we celebrate it with full awareness and appropriate preparation.

The word "sacrifice" comes to us from the Latin words "sacer" and "facere," meaning to make holy or sacred, to sanctify or consecrate. In our Judeo-Christian heritage, there is a tradition of what are called "sacrificial offerings" involving the setting aside of something valuable to honor God. Such sacrifices are prescribed throughout the Old Testament as signs of our dependence on God, as acts of thanksgiving, and as acts of reparation for turning away from God. Hundreds of verses in the Bible refer to the tribe of priests, the temple, the altar, the sacred vessels and vestments, the things to be offered, and to the proper attitude or inner disposition of the people. "No one," Deuteronomy 16:16 tells us, "shall appear before the Lord empty-handed."

That is important because sacrifice is the opposite of disobedience. Every sin is ultimately our saying "No" to God; it is an injustice because it is a refusal by us to honor God as God. But each prescribed sacrifice offered with sincerity expresses acceptance of and submission to the will of God — not because God needs that submission, but because *we* need it to be happy, to live in peace and love and joy.

Old Testament sacrifices were nearly always items of food. In the most common form of sacrifice, a portion was consumed by fire to show that the gift was truly passed from the sacrificer into the possession of God, while another portion was given to the priests, and a third portion was returned to the one who presented the gift for sacrifice. The portion returned, usually the meat of cattle, sheep, or goats, was then used for a holy meal, a joyful celebration with relatives and friends. The meal was shared with joy because their eating it together meant they were joined in submission to the will of God, celebrating in unity and in peace and in happy anticipation of the promised Savior.

Those sacrifices prefigured the perfect, promised sacrifice, the ultimate sacrifice, the sacrifice of Jesus Christ on the cross at Calvary, the sacrifice which repairs the breach caused by the sin of origin cited earlier. It is the sacrifice which opens us to unity with God and with each other, the central moment in all human history. The meaning of Christ's sacrifice is summed up in the Eucharist proclamation, "Lord, by your cross and resurrection, you have set us free. You are the Savior of the world."

In the Eucharistic celebration, the Holy Sacrifice of the Mass, the Church re-presents — not *represents*, meaning "to symbolize," but *re-presents*, meaning "to make present" — the sacrifice of Jesus Christ for the people of every age. Some persons misunderstand and misrepresent the Church's teaching and say that we claim to repeat Christ's sacrifice at Calvary in the Mass. No, that is wrong. Christ died once for all. Others think of it as a sort of "instant replay" of a past event at Calvary. No, that, too, is wrong. It might be helpful to understand the Church's teaching that Christ's sacrifice on the cross is made present for us at each Mass by considering what is happening in our physical universe. If you look at the sun this moment, what you are seeing is a violent explosion on the surface of the sun emitting light and heat — eight minutes ago. Traveling at the speed of light, what you see happening on the sun this moment would have been visible to someone half the distance from the sun four minutes ago. The explosion is not repeated when you see it and is not the "replay" of a past event when it reaches your eyes. You see the event as it occurs, but which, traveling at the speed of light, takes eight minutes to reach you on the planet Earth. That same event would be present to someone twice the distance from the sun eight minutes from now. It would not be repeated or "replayed" for the person twice the distance from the sun; it would simply be made present to that person at that time. The same is true of the starlight you see at night, except that is a process occurring over millions of years instead of just minutes.

The Holy Sacrifice of the Mass extends through time the moment when Christ is raised up on the cross to raise us up from the forces that drag us down and divide us. It is the moment when Jesus literally and figuratively fleshes out the unconditional love of God for each one of us. The suffering he endured to redeem us gives us an idea of how much we are loved. He was betrayed, tortured, and beaten. He suffered the agony in the garden where he asked twice to be spared: "My Father, if it is possible, let this cup pass from me; yet, not as I will, but as you will." (Matt. 26:39) and "Withdrawing a second time, he prayed again, 'My Father, if it is not possible that this cup pass without my drinking it, your will be done!'" (Matt. 26:42) He endured the scourging at the pillar, the crowning with thorns, the carrying of the cross, all of that horrible humiliation, pain, and grief. He was abandoned by all those crowds of people who followed him through Galilee, all those crowds of people who were there to cheer him on Palm Sunday when he came to Jerusalem, all those people who stood around while he was unjustly tried by the Sanhedrin and by the Romans and condemned by both, all those who mocked and jeered as he walked the way of the cross to Calvary, all those who deserted him at the end, all those who shouted, "Come down from that cross. Then we will follow you." All of that he endured to redeem us, to free us to be what we are created to be, to show us how much we are loved. And then again, at the end, he showed us how we are to love by his prayer for all, "Father, forgive them, they know not what they do."

Many react to all that by saying or thinking, "If I had been there, I would never have let Jesus suffer and die abandoned like that." In giving us himself in the Eucharist, the same Body and Blood that was poured out for us on the cross now in sacrament form, Jesus is telling us, "It's not too late. It's not too late." Every time the Mass is offered, we have the chance to be there for him. That is why the Church requires, obliges Catholics to assist at Mass on Sunday, the first day of the week, the day that celebrates the Lord's Resurrection which validates all that Jesus said and did. And that is why so many Catholics, deeply aware of the privilege that is theirs in receiving the Body and Blood of Christ, assist at Mass *every* day of the week. They realize God is present to us in many ways, in every place and time. He is present in creation and in every creature as the very Source of Life. He is present wherever "two or three are gathered" in his name. He is present in his Word, our Sacred Scriptures. He is present in the worshipping community gathered at the altar. But the most sacred presence of God for us is in the Body and Blood of Jesus Christ which he offered on the cross for our redemption and which he offers to us every day in the Eucharist at the Holy Sacrifice of the Mass.

Obeying his commission and his command to the Church to "do this" through all time for all generations is the most serious mission of the Church because this sacrament is its Most Precious Treasure. That is why the Mass is called the summit of the Church's activity, the fount from which all else flows — all of our teaching, missions, prayer, religious life, Scripture study, works of charity, acts of virtue, Church laws, holy marriage, and all the rest. Everything the Church does is intended to help us give ourselves to God in union with the supreme gift of Jesus on the cross. We are reminded of that at each Mass when the priest raises the bread and wine, now consecrated into the Body and Blood of Christ through the priestly power conveyed in the sacrament of Holy Orders, and says, "Through him, with him, and in him, in the unity of the Holy Spirit, all glory and honor is yours, almighty Father, for ever and ever." And we respond, "Amen."

As you might expect, the Church exercises great care in obeying its sacred commission and command. The Church brings the power of consecration — known more precisely in the catechism as transubstantiation — down through the ages and around the world by the ordination of priests in the sacrament of Holy Orders. The Church erects noble buildings and fashions dignified altars for our Eucharstic worship to express our deep respect for the presence of the Lord's Body and Blood and to help our perception and understanding. The Church requires those who receive Communion to be baptized members of the Church and to be instructed in the meaning of this sacrament. The Church asks communicants to show respect for this great gift by observing fasting requirements, by making our responses and singing our hymns at Mass with fervor, and by being punctual, attentive, prayerful, and suitably attired. Most important, the Church asks us to examine our consciences in the light of the Commandments and the laws of the Church to determine if we are free of serious sin that would make our reception of Communion a dishonor and an insult to our Lord — and, should we be aware of serious sin, to refrain from Communion until we have received our Lord's forgiveness in the Sacrament of Reconciliation.

Our reception of the Eucharist, our Holy Communion, brings us into a special union with our Lord and with each other, and that "common union" shapes our attitude toward others. We, all of us, are redeemed by the sacrifice of Christ, not because we merit it, but because he loves us, all of us, totally and unconditionally. Receiving his Body and Blood in Holy Communion is our sharing in that love. Sharing in that love, loving Christ, commits us to loving those Christ loves — every person in every place at every moment, starting with the people we see every day. We share that love by being present to them, anticipating their needs, rejoicing in their joy, suffering in their pain, and, when they hurt or disappoint us, by responding not with resentment or anger and bitterness, but with the forgiveness Christ expressed for all of us as he looked down from his cross and said, "Father, forgive them."

The Eucharist especially commits us to loving service of the poor, those who often, like Christ himself, have been abandoned, betrayed, and left desolate in a world of plenty. Remember that it is not just service to the poor alone which is to distinguish followers of Christ. It is *loving* service. The Eucharist, the Eucharistic spirit, helps us get away from the idea that the poor are a burden and we have to do something, so we just send them a check or put some food in a basket and have somebody take it to the church. The Eucharist preserves us from the attitude, "I will give them something, but I don't want to see them, I don't want to look at them, I don't want to touch them, I don't want to love them." If we truly cannot help personally because we do not have the strength or the resources to heal wounds and fix the hunger and cure the sickness, we can at least insist that it be done and help personally to the extent we are able. Journalists who interview the homeless and the poor, those enslaved by our welfare system, those in prison, the disadvantaged in general, often ask them what is the worst feature of their lives. Is it lack of material possessions? Oddly, they seldom say that. We think, "Oh, they have nothing, how can they live?" Well, that is our perspective, our view. Do they say lack of political power? No. That is what the leaders of various movements say, but it is not what the disadvantaged themselves say. What do the disadvantaged, the poor, the weak say is the worst feature of their lives? It is hopelessness. And providing *loving* care for the poor, living the Eucharistic spirit, makes us ambassadors of hope, helping in their spiritual as well as material need. Mother Teresa, who referred to America as one of the most spiritually impoverished nations of all despite our material wealth, often referred to the poor as "Christ in distressing disguise" and reminded us that, "At the end of life, we will not be judged by how many diplomas we have received, how much money we have made, how many great things we have done. We will be judged by 'I was hungry and you gave me to eat. I was naked and you clothed me. I was homeless and you took me in.' Hungry not only for bread, but hungry for love. Naked not only for clothing, but naked of human dignity and respect. Homeless not only for want of a room of bricks, but homeless because of rejection." The Eucharist keeps in mind for us Christ's words, "whatever you did for one of these least brothers of mine, you did for me," (Matt. 25:40) and strengthens us to help.

The Eucharist, the sacrament in which Christ is worshipped and his suffering and death are recalled, also is our greatest source of hope because it brings with it what the Church refers to as Christ's "pledge of future glory" — the medicine of immortality, the antidote for death. It may strike some as odd that Jesus gives us his pledge of everlasting life in the Eucharist — "I am the living bread that came down from heaven; whoever eats this bread will live forever." (John 6:51) — and then he himself proceeds to die in his agonizing crucifixion. Why? So that he may be "the firstborn from the dead" (Rev. 1:5 and Col. 1:18) and teach us in a way we would never forget that death is not the end, it is the end of the beginning. What does that mean? Well, death is one of the penalties for the sin of origin, original sin. The greatest penalty is the loss of the friendship of God, but there was also lost the freedom from illness and the freedom from ignorance and the freedom from death. God, in his providence, is restoring these things to us one by one. We are restored to the friendship of God by Baptism. Our science and art of medicine give us progressive freedom from illness. Our own intellect, given to us by God, frees us from ignorance.

The last enemy is death, and Jesus, by his conquest of death, has won for us everlasting life, our "pledge of future glory."

That is why the priest holds up the host for us just before communion and says with complete and utter confidence, "Happy are those who are called to his supper."

Cardinal Newman, many years ago wrote, "God so loved the world as to give his only begotten Son. He loved mankind in their pollution, in spite of the abhorrence with which the pollution filled him. He loved them with a Father's love, who does not cast off a worthless son once and for all, but is affectionate toward his person while he is indignant toward his misconduct. He loved them for what still remains in them of their original excellence, which was in its measure a reflection of his own. He loved them before he redeemed them and he redeemed them because he loved them."

"I Understand."

At the end of the Gospel of John, we are told, "There are also many other things that Jesus did, but if these were to be described individually, I do not think the whole world would contain the books that would be written." The same is true of any effort to describe the treasures made available to us through the Church. In these pages, a few of the basic, vital treasures have been introduced with the intention of providing a solid base from which you may launch or continue your own exploration and discover more, many more reasons for hope. The sacraments of healing and service, the guidance provided by the commandments and beatitudes, and our union with God and with each other in prayer have been left for our later consideration.

We began our visit with talk of human freedom. We have ended with talk of love. It is truly impossible in any relationship to have one without the other. But abuses of freedom have muddied the water for many in regard to the nature and power of God. The Church says God is love and God is omnipotent. The word "omnipotent" comes to us from the Latin "omnis," meaning all, and "potens," meaning powerful. "If God is love and God is all powerful," some ask, "why do we have so much evil and suffering in the world? It must mean either God is not loving or God is not all powerful."

Another writer, Dr. R. Davies, provides some insight for us: "Love is the power to grant freedom without desiring to limit or inhibit its exercise. It is the power to give freedom without any will to take it back." That power to refrain absolutely from trespassing or curtailing our freedom despite our misuse of it actually is a demonstration of God's power, God's omnipotence, "because only God can give and not take back," Davies writes. "He suffers within himself the entire consequence of allowing us absolute freedom. That is his love."

Later Davies concludes that, "the existence of evil and suffering in the world is a proof, not that God is either good but powerless or all powerful but not good. On the contrary, it is a proof that God is both loving and omnipotent. Only absolute love could grant unhindered freedom, and only omnipotence can endure the operation of that freedom."

Whether the operation of that freedom, our use of that freedom, increases evil and suffering or increases peace, love, and joy in the world always remains in our hands. We saw in Genesis that misuse or abuse of freedom left us with a legacy of enslavement to misery. Through the cross of Christ, the Church reminds us, we have been set free. But the questions each of us must answer now are, "What am I doing to stay free?" and "What am I doing for the freedom of others?" Each of us has a role to play, a responsibility in all this. Our lives have a purpose — a divine purpose. Each of us is called to make a difference, but we must choose to answer and act. We have available to us in the Church, I noted earlier, every help, every aid, every assistance, and every advantage to enable us to use our freedom wisely and well, to make a difference. But even when we falter or stumble in our human weakness, we are never abandoned, are never without hope.

There is an old story about a little boy who was passing by a pet shop and saw a pen full of puppies in the store. He went inside and sat by the pen. When the owner noticed him there, he walked over and asked the boy if he would like to have the pen opened so he could see the puppies better. The boy nodded and the owner opened the gate. Then all the little puppies came bounding and tumbling out to play, all of them except one that could not walk very well. One of his legs was damaged.

The boy asked the owner, "How much are they?" The owner told him, "Fifty dollars." The boy looked dejected and said, "I don't have that much money. All I have is $22.37. May I give you that and work off the rest?" The owner agreed and asked the boy which puppy he wanted. When the boy pointed at the puppy with a lame leg, the owner said, "Oh, you don't want that one. That one is damaged. Pick another one." "No," the boy said, "that's the one I want." The puzzled owner said, "You can have him for nothing. I'll just give him to you." But the boy answered, "No, he's worth every bit as much as the others." As the boy got up and walked around the counter to pay, the owner saw that he was wearing a brace and walking with a limp. He asked the boy, "Why do you want that one?" "Well," the boy said, "I understand him. He needs me."

The Church — with its sacraments, its Sacred Scripture, and Tradition — is Jesus ever present, ever repeating in every moment of every life, "I understand you. You need me." May our awareness of his understanding love fill us with hope, strengthen us in the exercise of our sacramental powers, free us from useless fear and anxiety, and help us grow together in grateful joy. Praised be Jesus Christ, now and forever.